100 answers to 100 questions

about How to Live Longer

Christian
LIFE
A STRANG COMPANY

Most CHRISTIAN LIFE products are available at special quantity discounts for bulk purchase for sales promotions, premiums, fund-raising, and educational needs. For details, write Christian Life, 600 Rinehart Road, Lake Mary, Florida 32746, or telephone (407) 333-0600.

100 Answers to 100 Questions about Living Longer
Published by Christian Life
A Strang Company
600 Rinehart Road
Lake Mary, Florida 32746
www.strang.com

Scripture quotations marked KJV are from the King James Version of the Bible

Scripture quotations marked NAS are from the New American Standard Bible. Copyright © 1960, 1962, 1963, 1968, 1971, 1972, 1973, 1975, 1977 by the Lockman Foundation. Used by permission. (www.Lockman.org)

Scripture quotations marked NIV are from the Holy Bible, New International Version. Copyright © 1973, 1978, 1984, International Bible Society. Used by permission.

Scripture quotations marked NKJV are from the New King James Version of the Bible. Copyright © 1979, 1980, 1982 by Thomas Nelson, Inc., publishers. Used by permission.

Scripture quotations marked NLT are from the Holy Bible, New Living Translation, copyright © 1996. Used by permission of Tyndale House Publishers, Inc., Wheaton, IL 60189. All rights reserved.

Cover design by Whisner Design Group, Tulsa, Oklahoma

Copyright © 2009 by Janet Maccaro, PhD, CNC
All rights reserved

ISBN 10: 1-59979-756-9
ISBN 13: 978-1-59979-756-4
BISAC Category: RELIGION/Christian Life/Personal Growth

First Edition

09 10 11 12 13 — 9 8 7 6 5 4 3 2 1

Printed in the United States of America

Contents

The Mind

The Spirit

Introduction

You can add up the statistics on average life spans and speculate about factors in the aging process and the biological limits of life, but what does that tell you about *your* life?

Each of us is given a predetermined number of days on this earth. Each one of these days is a gift. How are you treating this precious gift? Are you disrespecting it by not caring for your body or nurturing your soul? Or are you living consciously realizing that you have a responsibility to be the very best expression of life that you can be?

At the end of our days, all of us want to have run the good race and to have fought the good fight. We want to have made a difference while on our earthly journey. We want to leave a "footprint" as proof that we were alive and that we mattered to those we loved, a "heart print" so to speak.

This is where stewardship comes in. What will you do with your appointed days? Will you embrace each one, the good and bad, the dark with the bright? Each day, whatever the circumstance, is given to teach you, grow you, mature and refine you, bring you joy, and give you the ability to be compassionate, loving, and forgiving. In other words, you are being "fired" in the "kiln of life." How will you come forth at the end? Will you come to the end of your days with a life as beautiful as the finest of porcelain? Or will you instead arrive cracked and broken, lacking a testimony or legacy of happiness?

If you look back on your life and see that you haven't lived it the best, you can begin right now to experience a richer life filled with better health, more even emotions, and a deeper spiritual walk. I am going to give you one hundred answers to your questions about how to not only live longer but also live better at any stage and any age. You will learn ways to bring health to your earthly frame, ways to heal your emotions, and ways to bring you closer to your Creator.

I am going to teach you how to embrace what is right and to discard what is stealing your vibrancy. These one hundred answers will be laid out for you in three sections: the body, the mind, and the spirit.

In the first section, I will offer you sixty answers to dietary questions and health recommendations that will help to lengthen your days. Read the "Life-Extender Tip" and implement it. By the end of the first sixty questions and answers, you will be armed with some of the best health-building tips of our time. As a result, you will have increased energy, greater relaxation, more restful sleep, better sex, and fewer ailments.

As we move into the second section, I will address twenty questions about emotions. These tips will help you to turn on your "inner light," ignite love, and allow your heart to focus again on possibilities, not problems. An unhealthy mind can lead to an unhealthy body. Science now confirms it! It has been said that each of us can choose to live in a "garden or a jungle." If we take responsibility for our emotions, we can truly change our mental environment and live a longer, more balanced, rewarding, and peaceful life.

In the third section, I will give you answers to some of life's most trying questions—those that involve your spirit. Do you live in fear of what the future might bring? Have you ever been hurt by someone you have trusted? Have you found yourself struggling to pray? Have you ever been angry with God?

God designed us to be His friends, but in our human ways, we often decide to "go it alone." When we choose to do this, we lack the wisdom and energy His friendship offers. If you remain in God and He is in you, your life experience becomes markedly different from the experience of those who do not have trust in God.

As you read this book, I want you to think about it as more than just answers to commonly asked questions; think about these as one hundred ways to extend your life as *you* find balance, love, peace, joy, and everything you need to make the rest of your life the best of your life—from health to eternity!

Can Ayurveda help me? How do I start?

Ayurveda is a five-thousand-year-old system from India of building health that focuses on eating fresh ingredients. The foods included in this way of eating are low fat, heart healthy, and packed with cancer-fighting antioxidants and phytochemicals. The principles of Ayurveda are beneficial because they promote a healthy balance of the mind, body, and spirit to produce optimal health and longevity.

answer

Ayurveda focuses on eating from a wide variety of foods to promote hormonal balance and boost the immune system.[1] To achieve this balance, you would need to eat from all six of the "tastes" to get the most benefit and antiaging protection. The six tastes include:

1. Bitter (green and yellow vegetables)
2. Sour (citrus and tomatoes)
3. Salty (fish and soy sauce)
4. Sweet (fruits and low-fat dairy products)
5. Pungent (ginger, peppers, and onions)
6. Astringent (beans, apples, and berries)

Additional nutraceuticals that have specific healing properties include:

▶ Garlic and onions to boost the immune system, helping to prevent colds

▶ Basil, cumin, and turmeric to help to prevent cancer of the bladder and prostate

▶ Black pepper, jalapeños, hot red peppers, and mustard to boost your metabolism for several hours (This helps to burn fat!)

▶ Cinnamon to help metabolize sugar, keeping your blood sugar levels steady

Ayurveda also stresses the importance of how and when you eat. All meals should be eaten in a relaxed atmosphere without intrusion, be it the television, newspaper, or going over the worries of the day. You should concentrate on the food itself and the company you are dining with.

Ayurveda places emphasis on identifying one's own constitutional type: vata, pitta, or kapha. They are similar to what we recognize in Western medicine as fat, thin, or muscular body types, but Ayurveda prescribes an eating plan to bring balance to all three types that promotes health and longevity.

A vata is usually thin, intuitive, anxious, vivacious, enthusiastic, imaginative, and tends toward constipation, cramps, and nervous disorders.

A pitta is usually medium build, intense and orderly, short-tempered, punctual, warm, loving, perfectionist, intelligent, and tends toward ulcers, heartburn, and hemorrhoids.

A kapha is usually heavyset, slow, relaxed, graceful, compassionate, forgiving, tolerant, affectionate, and tends toward high cholesterol, obesity, sinus problems, and allergies.

I do not personally ascribe to the religious aspects of Ayurveda, but its principles are timeless.

Knowing your constitutional type, you can:

▶ Take the right measures to restore balance
▶ Prevent disease
▶ Extend length and quality of your life

life-extender tip

Choose today to eat slowly, and stop when you are full. Begin designing your meals using the "six tastes."

2

How much fiber do I need, and what are the best sources?

The proper amount of fiber in your diet is important for maintaining bulk that is required for healthy digestive function. Fiber, which is an essential carbohydrate food component, also helps to maintain cholesterol levels that are already in the normal range as well as clean the walls of the intestines and enhance the elimination of fecal mutagens. The addition of dietary fiber to your diet can lessen certain health risk factors such as colon cancer, irritable bowel syndrome, and diverticulitis.

answer

People who get at least 25 grams of fiber daily have a real age that is up to three years younger than those who get the national average of 12 grams daily.[2] Eating fiber early in the day is very helpful because it prevents spikes in blood sugar that can damage arteries and increase the risk of fatty buildup and heart disease. Eat fiber at breakfast to slow the rate at which your stomach empties. It will also increase your feeling of fullness so that you won't want to snack and eat excessive calories throughout the rest of the day.

Fiber is a term for the indigestible components of the plant foods we eat. The intestines of people who eat a lot of fiber function better, since fiber increases the bulk and frequency of bowel movements. Constipation is often caused by a lack of fiber. Fiber also aids digestion by promoting the growth of "good" intestinal flora.

In addition, fiber may help you to lose weight due to the fact that its bulking activity makes you feel fuller faster. Therefore you may eat less.

Other sources of fiber to add to your diet are as follows:

▶ Whole grains (bran cereal, whole-wheat bread)
▶ Fruits and vegetables
▶ Powdered fiber supplement (from psyllium seed husks)

Note: When adding fiber to the diet, be sure to drink plenty of water! Not doing so may result in intestinal pain or blockage. If suffering from hemorrhoids, use fiber with care. Do not use fiber if you have undiagnosed abdominal pain or nausea, or if vomiting is present.

Fiber in the amount of 25 grams each day promotes:

▶ Better blood sugar control
▶ Improved heart disease risk
▶ Lower appetite due to feeling full
▶ Reduced constipation and reduced risk of colon cancer, irritable bowel syndrome, and diverticulitis

life-extender tip

Have oatmeal for breakfast! Choose to eat fiber early in the day.

3

Can you explain the
importance of omega-3
fatty acids?

Omega-3 fatty acids are found in cold-water fish such as salmon, tuna, herring, mackerel, and whitefish, and in other nutrients like perilla and flaxseed oil. They can also be taken as supplements in capsule form.

answer

Your body needs fatty acids to survive and is able to make all but two of them—linoleic acid and linolenic acid. These two fatty acids must be supplied by our diets and are therefore considered essential fatty acids (EFAs).

EFAs help protect blood vessels from excessive plaque buildup, reduce inflammation throughout the body by stimulating the production of leukotrienes (which are natural compounds that inhibit inflammation), prevent high blood pressure, and help contribute to respiratory health.

Udo's Choice Perfected Oil Blend (available at most health food stores) is a capsule supplement of omega-3 fatty acids that you can take if you don't consume enough fatty acids in your regular diet. It is a blend of natural unrefined oils and nutritional cofactors designed to meet your body's daily requirements of all essential fatty acids. Two capsules (1000 mg) three times daily are suggested. Take with meals, but *not* with fiber supplements!

There is mounting evidence that suggests that supplementation with omega-3 fatty acids, as well as increased consumption of fruits and vegetables, significantly decreases the chances of developing dementia or Alzheimer's disease.[3]

The goal here is to consume all of the omega-3 oils that you can because of their far-reaching health benefits. Omega-3 each day keeps many illnesses at bay! The American Heart Association published a study of 11,323 heart attack survivors showing that those who took 1,000 mg of fish oil supplements every day were 45 percent less likely to be dead at the end of 3.5 years.[4]

Note: If you are taking anticoagulant drugs like Coumadin (or warfarin), you should inform your doctor that you are considering implementing a regimen of EFAs to your life-extending protocol. An adjustment may have to be made in your medication since fatty acids may thin the blood and can interfere with blood clotting.

Populations getting ample omega-3 fatty acids experience:

▶ The least cardiovascular disease
▶ The highest percentage of healthy and robust seniors

life-extender tip

Add omega-3 fatty acids to your diet. Here's how: take one 1,000 mg fish oil capsule or have fish for dinner tonight. You may also take flaxseed or perilla oil.

question

4

Which antioxidants should I take?

Oxidative damage and the resultant inflammatory changes are now known to lie at the root of most common chronic conditions, such as cardiovascular disease and cancer, in humans.[5] Antioxidants come to the rescue! Antioxidants are a specific group of vitamins, minerals, or other substances that neutralize free radicals, thereby preventing damage to your cells. After they neutralize or "quench" these free radials, they become inactive and are eliminated from your body. This means that you continually need to supply your body with antioxidant protection through your diet, supplementation, or both.

answer

All experts agree that eating whole foods in their natural state complete with naturally occurring antioxidants is the best way to go. But in this fast-paced society, most of us need to resort to supplementation to insure that we are covered. This does not mean that you should not make an effort to eat fresh and healthy.

Because of their ability to prevent many of the diseases associated with aging, three major antioxidants—beta-carotene and vitamins C and E—should be added to your arsenal of life extenders. These three antioxidants offer a three-point attack when it comes to preventing oxidative damage.

Beta-carotene quenches single oxygen molecules. Vitamin C protects tissues and blood components, while vitamin E protects cell membranes. When taken together in symphony, they "mop up" free radicals as they form and before they do damage to our systems.

Vitamin E is an antioxidant derived from plants. It is a family of nutrients that include tocopherol and tocotrienols, each with their own subfamilies of alpha, beta, gamma, and delta substances. Unless the brand of vitamin E you take contains the full spectrum of these nutrients, you will not get the full benefits of vitamin E.

Vitamin C and beta-carotene also fight free radicals and offer protection against heart disease, cataracts, and certain cancers, including skin cancer.

Antioxidant Food Sources		
Vitamin C	**Vitamin E**	**Beta-carotene**
Mangoes	Mangoes	Mangoes
Sweet potatoes	Sweet potatoes	Sweet potatoes
Papayas	Almonds	Green leafy vegetables
Red, green, yellow peppers	Avocados	
Broccoli	Walnuts	
Strawberries	Sunflower seeds	
Orange juice	Wheat germ	
	Peanut butter	

Triple play: Mangoes (no other tropical fruit contains all three!) and sweet potatoes are rich sources of all three of these antiagers.

Experts agree—add these three:

▶ Vitamin E: Natural vitamin E is absorbed more efficiently than synthetic vitamin E. The daily recommended dose is 400 international units (IU) of natural vitamin E.

▶ Vitamin C: Take 500–1000 mg two to three times daily.

▶ Beta-carotene: Take 25,000 IU daily.

life-extender tip

Add these three antioxidants to your regimen: beta-carotene and vitamins C and E.

5 Should I take digestive enzymes?

As we age, pancreatic enzyme levels decline, diminishing our ability to break down food. Enzymes are vital to maintain cellular function and optimal health. By taking an enzyme formula with each meal, you are assisting your body to facilitate digestion. Enzymes are essential to the body's absorption and full use of food. The primary digestive enzymes are protease (to digest protein), amylase (to digest carbohydrates), and lipase (to digest fat). These enzymes function as biological catalysts to help break down food. Raw foods also provide enzymes that naturally break down food for proper absorption. Our capacity to make enzymes diminishes with age, which often results in challenges to our digestive system.

answer

Because of today's hectic lifestyles, we often overcook, microwave, and overprocess our foods, killing all or most of the naturally occurring enzymes. While it is true that we occasionally eat raw foods that do contain live enzyme activity, our consumption of cooked "enzyme-depleted" foods is greater. This in turn leaves our bodies with the big task of producing more enzymes to break down these cooked foods. That is, unless we supplement.

I know of people who report more energy and weight loss, better sleep, less hunger, an overall feeling of well-being complete with less bloating, and less or no need for antacids or medications that treat gastrointestinal disorders after implementing an enzyme program. It is important that you use an enzyme supplement tailored to your particular needs.

Most people do very well on a broad-spectrum enzyme supplement.

A deficiency of any two or more enzymes can lower the quality of your life because of lowered immune response. In fact, according to DicQie Fuller, PhD, DSc, author of *The Healing Power of Enzymes*, it is almost certain that an enzyme depletion exists anytime we suffer from an acute or chronic illness![6]

Enzymes have far-reaching benefits. They deliver nutrients, carry away toxic wastes, digest food, purify the blood, deliver hormones by feeding and fortifying the endocrine system, balance cholesterol and triglyceride levels, feed the brain, and cause *no* harm to the body.

As an added bonus, enzymes can fight the aging process by increasing blood supply to the skin, delivering nutrients, and then carrying away waste products that can make your skin look old, tired, and wrinkled.

As we age, our enzyme supply dwindles. This is why I have always said, "Enzymes—if you don't make them, take them!"

Avoid these three basic types of enzyme deficiencies:

▶ A deficiency of protease limits your ability to digest proteins.

▶ A deficiency of lipase limits your ability to digest fats.

▶ A deficiency of amylase affects your ability to digest carbohydrates.

life-extender tip

Take two capsules of a plant-source comprehensive enzyme supplement with each meal.

question

6 Can taking a statin medication deplete my body of CoQ_{10}?

Now recommended by many cardiologists, coenzyme Q_{10} is a powerful antioxidant that occurs naturally in all the cells of your body and helps the heart function more efficiently. In Japan, Europe, and Israel, coenzyme Q_{10} is a popular cardioprotective supplement. If you are taking a statin medication, it is imperative that you take coenzyme Q_{10} because the statins deplete the body of this vital substance that is essential for degenerative conditions, fatigue, and muscle weakness.

answer

A study of heart attack patients showed that when compared to a placebo, supplementation with CoQ_{10} (120 mg daily) reduced secondary cardiac events by 45 percent *and* significantly reduced the number of cardiac deaths!

Many of these heart attack patients were prescribed a statin drug to lower cholesterol levels. The major adverse effect of statin treatment was fatigue that occurred in 40.8 percent of the placebo group, whereas only 6.8 percent of the patients taking CoQ_{10} experienced fatigue.[7]

As we age, we produce only 50 percent of the CoQ_{10} that we did in our younger days. This makes CoQ_{10} supplementation one of the most important nutrient supplementation for people over the age of thirty. In addition, since our cells need CoQ_{10} for energy production, the result of a CoQ_{10} deficit can be seen in a greater incidence of age-related disorders.

It was more than thirty years ago that Dr. Karl Folkers, a biochemical scientist at the University of Texas in Austin, discovered that coenzyme Q_{10} helps to strengthen the heart muscle and energize the cardiovascular system in many heart patients. Studies have revealed that CoQ_{10} may protect against atherosclerosis, and it has been shown to have anti-oxidant properties against the formation of oxysterols.[8]

While it is true that our hearts are often adversely affected by a CoQ_{10} deficiency, increasing evidence indicates that our brain may be even more adversely affected by an inadequate supply of CoQ_{10}.

Dietary sources for CoQ_{10} include salmon, sardines, mackerel, peanuts, spinach, and beef.

CoQ_{10} has been found to:

▶ Promote cardiovascular health

▶ Prevent premature aging of the skin

▶ Benefit the immune system

▶ Improve cognitive, nerve, cellular, and cranial vascular health

▶ Protect against periodontal or gum problems

life-extender tip

Take 100 mg of coenzyme Q_{10} (ubiquinone) daily.

question

7 Are there natural remedies for my sleepless nights?

Sleep is a supreme tonic. Sleeping soundly is vital to our well-being because it is only during rest that our bone marrow and lymph nodes produce substances to empower our immune systems. It is during the beginning of our sleep cycle that much of the body's repair work is done. Asian medicine recognizes the importance of sleep, even suggesting that one hour of sleep before midnight is worth two hours of sleep after midnight, in terms of healing and regenerating the body.

answer

Because some medication that aids sleep can be habit-forming or addictive, the following four natural substances may help to lull you to sleep, thereby helping your body repair, regenerate, and rejuvenate safely and effectively without fear of side effects or addiction.

1. Passionflower relaxes the mind and muscles.
2. Melatonin is an antioxidant hormone. Studies have shown that a nightly melatonin supplement boosts the performance during sleep of immune systems compromised by age, drugs, or stress. It helps to keep us in rhythm with the day and the seasons. It plays a large role in reducing sleep disorders.
3. 5HTP is the step between tryptophan and serotonin. 5HTP is converted to serotonin. It is nonaddictive and serves as a "natural tranquilizer" for restful sleep.
4. Magnesium counteracts stress and is a critical mineral necessary for good nerve and muscle function, and so much more. It is a very important mineral to consider for restful sleep!

Guidelines for better sleep:

▶ Avoid caffeine (colas, teas, and chocolate) and alcohol before bedtime.

▶ Avoid large meals, and limit fluid intake before bed so that you are not trying to digest a large meal or having to make trips to the bathroom during the night.

▶ Avoid highly engaging activities. Don't watch dramatic television shows or do work close to bedtime. Keep the television and computer out of your bedroom.

▶ Avoid sharing your bed with a pet. Cats and dogs can be cuddly in bed, but sharing a bed with your pet can be disruptive.

▶ Think dark! At bedtime, it is lights out! Try light-blocking curtains or even a sleep mask.

▶ Make sure your bed is large enough to give you and your partner room to move around. Replace that old uncomfortable mattress with a new one that fits you and your partner best.

life-extender tip

Sleep deep! Take the steps needed today to insure a good night's sleep!

question

8 Why are "green drinks" so popular?

For centuries, civilizations have understood the value of green foods such as chlorella, spirulina, and cereal grasses such as wheat and barley. In our modern times, scientists are rediscovering the many benefits of these green "superfoods" that contain the highest levels of easily digestible vegetable proteins, amino acids, carotenoids, vitamin B_{12}, iron, trace minerals, and the essential fatty acids GLA and DHA, as well as polysaccharides chlorophyll and sulfolipids.

answer

Dr. Norman Walker, a centenarian health researcher who was known for his vast knowledge on the subject of juicing, lived primarily on fruit and vegetable juices for over sixty years. He felt that his longevity was due in part to the liquid oxygen he received from the chlorophyll contained in fresh juices.

One of the *most* effective tools for building your health is found in the plant kingdom. Green superfoods are just that—SUPER—when it comes to being *super*charged with nutrition. They are nutritionally more concentrated and potent than regular greens like salads and green vegetables.

Greens are far and away our most important food source. They provide us with all of the essential components of health. They are our food as well as our medicine. Where green plants do not grow, we cannot live!

Chlorophyll is the "blood" of all plant life. It is the protein that resembles the molecules of human red blood cells. Chlorophyll has been compared to hemoglobin molecules—the oxygen carrier in human blood—and shown to be almost identical.

By adding green superfoods or juices to your diet, you are adding vital age-extending nutrients such as enzymes, minerals, oxygen, vitamins, and protein to your blood!

Chlorella is the richest source of chlorophyll and contains over 60 percent protein. This freshwater alga even surpasses plant life in terms of being a virtual powerhouse of nutrients. In addition to its higher-than-plant-life content of chlorophyll and high amounts of protein, chlorella also houses eight essential amino acids. In addition, it contains RNA and DNA, which are the nucleic acids that govern cell growth, reproduction, and repair. Chlorella is also a source of vitamins C, B_1, B_2, B_6, B_{12}, E, and K; niacin; beta-carotene; pantothenic acid; folic acid; biotin; choline; inositol; PABA; and minerals such as calcium, potassium, copper, zinc, and iron.

Chlorophyll:

► Purifies the liver and neutralizes toxins in the body
► Is a natural antibacterial that can be used inside and outside the body
► Provides an antimutagenic power thought to inhibit and reduce the formation of cancers in humans

life-extender tip

Add green foods or green juices to your diet today: chlorella, barley grass, wheatgrass, spirulina, blue and blue-green algae, or a powdered combination of all of these found at any local health food store! Make a "green drink" today!

9 Will a massage really help me de-stress?

Do you want an easy way to release both stored physical and emotional tension? Massage is *the* answer! Why not schedule a massage today? Massage aids in relaxation, gives relief from pain, and provides increased range of motion. In recent days, massage studios have opened up in just about every city in America and are doing *very* well. It goes to show that America is stressed and looking for relief! Why not join the hundreds of thousands of people in this country who already know that massage is just what the doctor ordered when it comes to relaxation of the body and mind?

answer

Massage therapy has been a recognized healing modality for thousands of years. The ancient Romans and Greeks used massage regularly as a healing treatment. In our day, massage therapy has become respected as a viable health discipline.

There is increasing demand for therapeutic massage. It is part of a huge trend toward health care with a mind, body, and spirit approach. It has become an integral part of health care and is used extensively in the offices of orthopedic doctors, chiropractors, and physical therapists.

Deep tissue and lymphatic drainage massage is a wonderful detoxification therapy, promoting elimination and drainage of mucus and fluid from the lungs.

Massage, once thought of as a luxury, is now affordable. The far-reaching healing effects are undeniable. With this in mind, you can't afford not to book a massage today!

Note: Massage is *not* recommended in cases of cancer, high fever, infection, high blood pressure, phlebitis, diabetes, cysts, or bruises. In these cases, check with your health-care provider.

What can massage do for you?

▶ It helps correct poor posture from spinal curvatures and whiplash.

▶ It helps chronic inflammatory conditions by increasing limbic circulation, especially swelling from sports injuries.

▶ It helps chronic fatigue syndrome and the muscle soreness of fibromyalgia.

▶ It is helpful for pain control, stimulating the production of endorphins, the body's natural pain relievers. It is especially effective for back and shoulder pain and spinal/nerve problems.

▶ It improves blood circulation throughout the body.

▶ It helps to relieve headaches and temporomandibular joint syndrome (TMJ).

▶ It helps to break up adhesions and scar tissue.

▶ It aids digestive disorders, chronic fatigue, cardiovascular disorders, and gynecological problems.

life-extender tip

Stress got you down? Schedule a massage today!

question

10 With it being a "cure-all," how do I work garlic into my diet?

Garlic's healing potential has been recognized for thousands of years. Throughout history, it has been used to treat everything from wounds and infections to digestive complaints. During World War II, when Russians ran out of penicillin for their battle wounds, they requisitioned garlic cloves, which is where garlic got its famous nickname "Russian penicillin."

answer

The chemistry and pharmacology of garlic are well studied. There are over one thousand research papers to prove it! Recent reports by the National Cancer Institute, on a large population of subjects in China, indicate that the consumption of garlic and other members of the *allium* genus (onions, leeks, and shallots) may help lower the incidence of stomach cancer.[9]

Here's why. Allicin, the active ingredient in garlic, may prevent atherosclerosis and coronary blockage, lower cholesterol, reduce blood clot formation, prevent yeast overgrowth, stimulate the pituitary, regulate blood sugar, and prevent cancer, particularly in the gastrointestinal tract. In addition, it is antibacterial, antifungal, and may often be used to treat minor infections.

Going further, garlic contains at least twenty-five germ-killing compounds and fights off bacterial, fungal, and even viral infections. It has been shown to have the ability to aid certain immune functions, particularly increasing the activity of natural killer cells.[10]

Garlic's benefits aren't seen only in the laboratory. People in southern Italy, who eat a lot of garlic, develop less stomach cancer than those Italians who live to their north (who typically do not eat much, if any, garlic).

This pungent bulb was prescribed by the fifth-century Greek physician Hippocrates as a cure-all in an ancient Sanskrit manuscript. Time tested, wouldn't you say?

Get the best garlic has to offer by:

▶ Enjoying it fresh—crushed garlic contains allicin, a compound that breaks down into a cascade of healthful compounds.

▶ Eating for convenience—raw, cooked, powdered; the choice is yours. All forms have their benefits!

▶ Cutting it fine—whether you cook it or eat it raw, mincing, crushing, or pressing it will vastly expand its surface area and give you the maximum number of healthful compounds.

▶ Taking it as a liquid extract—you will find it at your local health food store. Just follow the label directions.

life-extender tip

Add garlic to your diet. Cook with it, roast it, or add liquid garlic extract to your favorite vegetable juice or salad dressing. Note: odorless liquid garlic extract called Kyolic (by Wakunaga of North America) is also available.

question

11 How much green tea should I drink to get the benefits?

The polyphenols in tea, especially the catechins, are powerful anti-oxidants that help ward off diabetes and cancer. The free-radical inhibiting property of tea is more potent than that of vitamin E and is a proven preventative and treatment for atherosclerosis, otherwise known as hardening of the arteries. Green tea has a four-thousand-year history of treating a wide variety of ailments. Chinese people have been touting the benefits of green tea since before the first dynasty.

answer

As early as 1944, an article was published by the National Cancer Institute that showed that a regular diet that included green tea could reduce the risks of esophageal cancer by as much as 60 percent. The study also found that certain compounds found in green tea tended to inhibit the growth of cancer cells.

Here are some of the most noteworthy cancer studies on green tea that I want to share with you:

When non-Hodgkin's lymphoma cells were transplanted into mice, green tea prevented 50 percent of the tumors from taking hold and significantly inhibited growth of the tumors that did manifest.[11]

Chronic atrophic gastritis is known to be an intermediate stage in the development of stomach cancer. Green tea was shown to help protect against the progression of atrophic gastritis in Japanese men.[12]

One clinical trial is currently under way at the M. D. Anderson Cancer Center in collaboration with Memorial Sloan-Kettering Cancer Center. This study will examine the safety and possible efficacy of consuming the equivalent of ten cups of green tea per day.[13]

What makes green tea so good for you? It is the fact that it is high in an antioxidant known as epigallocatechin gallate, or EGCG for short.[14]

Two to three cups per day should provide you with many benefits. No time for a tea party? Try green tea capsules instead!

Clinical tests show that EGCG:

▶ Inhibits the growth of new cancer cells but kills some existing cancer cells without harming normal cells

▶ Inhibits the unnatural formation of blood clots, which have been known to cause thrombosis, one of the leading causes of heart attacks and stroke

▶ Reduces total cholesterol levels and increases the ratio of HDL (good cholesterol) to LDL (bad cholesterol)

life-extender tip

Have a cup of green tea today!

question

12
Will eating nuts help prevent heart disease?

Studies show that frequently eating nuts dramatically improves health by significantly lowering the risk of heart disease. A group of researchers at Loma Linda University in California performed a study on 31,000 white Californian Seventh-Day Adventists in 1992. The study, referred to as the Adventist Health Study, reported that those persons who ate nuts daily had up to 60 percent fewer heart attacks than those who ate nuts less than once per month.[15] Daily nut consumption benefited everyone in the study—men, women, vegetarians, meat eaters, people who were overweight and those who were thin or at their ideal weight, old or young, those who exercised regularly and those who did not. Benefits were also noted in another study for African Americans as well.[16]

answer

Choose any or a combination of the following: almonds, peanuts, walnuts, pistachios, pecans, Brazil nuts, cashews, hazelnuts, macadamias, and chestnuts. Just a handful of nuts can do so much for your health! Studies have confirmed that the health benefit of eating nuts not only positively affects cardiovascular health, but it also lowers the risk of stroke, type 2 diabetes, dementia, macular degeneration, and gallstones.

It has been calculated that daily nut eaters gain an extra five to six years of life free from coronary artery disease and that nut eating appears to increase longevity by about two years.[17] Studies suggest that 1 to 2 ounces of nuts should be consumed daily to gain the maximum benefits these little "powerhouses" of nutrition provide. Fiber, vitamin E, folic acid, copper, magnesium, and the amino acid arginine all contribute to a decreased risk of heart disease and can be found in a handful of nuts!

Here's more. The protein content of nuts is around 10–25 percent, which makes them a great alternative to meat as a source of protein. And because it is plant protein, there's no cholesterol and very little saturated fat involved.

You should, for all of these health-promoting reasons, incorporate nuts into your life-extension protocol: pecans, pistachios, almonds, Brazil nuts, cashews, hazelnuts, walnuts, macadamias, chestnuts, and peanuts. The choice is yours!

Nuts really can:

► Lower your cholesterol
► Reduce your risk of heart disease, cancer, stroke, and diabetes
► Help to keep your weight in check

life-extender tip

Eat a handful of nuts today!

13 Should I add "power mushrooms" to my diet?

It's time for Americans to learn what the Chinese and Japanese have known for generations. For three thousand years, Asians have enjoyed the power mushrooms not only for their taste but also for their therapeutic value. In fact, Chinese legend is filled with stories of people who discovered a one-thousand-year-old mushroom and became immortal! But seriously, you are reading these one hundred answers so that you can learn how to extend *your* days, and while these mushrooms do not promise immortality, they certainly provide you with polysaccharides, sterols, coumarin, vitamins, minerals, and amino acids that can do wonders for your health.

answer

▼

Today, there are about thirty-five different species of mushrooms that we can partake of. Most of them are edible and have medicinal properties. Scientists are now discovering what natural healers have known for centuries. Not only are mushrooms important sources of nutrients that stimulate the immune system, but also researchers say that they possibly help fight cancer, high cholesterol, and perhaps even the AIDS virus.

America's favorite mushroom, "the button," was never thought to have much medicinal value, but recent studies have found that this little mushroom packs quite a punch when it comes to preventing breast cancer![18] Other forms of mushrooms were also found to help prevent breast cancer. White stuffing mushrooms offered the strongest amount of protection, followed by shiitake, portobello, cremini, and baby button. All of these mushrooms showed a significant effect, whether eaten raw or cooked.

I should mention here that while raw mushrooms are a favorite at most salad bars, do not make a habit of eating too many uncooked mushrooms. Raw mushrooms contain hydrazines, which are toxic chemicals. Since no one is quite sure of just how many raw mushrooms you would have to eat in order to enter a "danger zone," I recommend that you cook all of your mushrooms because hydrazines are eliminated during the heating process. For both taste and nutrition, mushrooms are better cooked. This is because they are mostly water. When you cook them, you remove the water and concentrate both the nutrients and the flavor!

In addition to maitake, shiitake, and reishi, you may want to try oyster, morel, porcini, cremini, and portobello. All of these mushrooms offer you far-reaching health benefits.

Add them to soups and casseroles, or toss them into a stir-fry. Be creative!

Mushrooms are known to:

- ▶ Boost immune function
- ▶ Lower bad cholesterol
- ▶ Regulate blood sugar
- ▶ Protect your body from viruses and possibly cancer by inhibiting tumor growth

life-extender tip

Add shiitake, maitake, or reishi mushrooms to your meal.

question

14 What are the benefits of lycopene?

Lycopene, a carotenoid without provitamin A activity, is a red, fat-soluble pigment found in many fruits, vegetables, plants, and microorganisms. It serves as an accessory light-gathering pigment and protects these organisms against the toxic effects of oxygen and light. Epidemiological studies have shown that high intake of lycopene-containing vegetables is inversely associated with the incidence of certain types of cancer.

answer

Tomatoes are *the* richest source of lycopene.[19] Have a glass of tomato juice, make a fabulous tomato sauce, or have a healthy slice of pizza with plenty of pizza sauce!

Tomato sauce—including ketchup, tomato juice, and pizza sauce—is the richest source of lycopene in the American diet, accounting for greater than 80 percent of the total lycopene intake of Americans. Processed tomatoes (canned tomatoes, tomato sauce, ketchup) contain more lycopene than unprocessed tomatoes because cooking breaks down cell walls, releasing and concentrating carotenoids.

Habitual intake of tomato products has been associated with the lowered risk of cancer of the digestive tract among Italians. In one six-year study by Harvard Medical School and Harvard School of Public Health, the diets of more than forty-seven thousand men were studied. Of forty-six fruits and vegetables evaluated, only the tomato products (which contain lycopene) showed a measurable relationship to a lowered risk of prostate cancer. As consumption of tomato products increased, levels of lycopene in the blood increased, and the risk of prostate cancer decreased. The study showed that heat processing of tomato products increased lycopene's bioavailability, meaning that it was more easily absorbed by the body.

Lycopene is deposited in the liver, lungs, prostate, colon, and skin. Its concentration in body tissues tends to be higher than all other carotenoids.

Lycopene is a proven antioxidant that neutralizes free radicals that damage the body's cells. It is a carotenoid that imparts red color not only to the bright red tomato but also to guava, watermelon, and pink grapefruit!

Ongoing research suggests that lycopene is associated with reduced risk of:

▶ Macular degeneration

▶ Serum lipid oxidation

▶ Cancers of the lung, bladder, cervix, and skin

life-extender tip
Add lycopene-rich foods to your diet today!

15

Why should I make the switch to sea salt?

You have probably heard that your body is 75 percent water. What you probably did not know is that the water contained in all your tissues, cells, and blood is a salty solution very similar to seawater. As John F. Kennedy once said, "All of us have in our veins the exact same percentage of salt in our blood that exists in the ocean, and, therefore, we have salt in our blood, in our sweat, in our tears. We are tied to the ocean. And when we go back to the sea…we are going back from whence we came."[20]

answer

In today's world, we have been often told that salt is not good for our health, but studies are finding what ancient cultures knew all along. Water and salt—sea salt, that is—are the very "essence of life." There is a very big difference between table salt and sea salt.

Over the years, with the advent of industrialized development, natural salt was "chemically cleaned" and reduced to a combination of sodium and chloride. Essential minerals and trace elements were removed as impurities. Sodium chloride (table salt) is an unnatural, isolated, unwholesome substance having very little in common with sea salt. Similar to white, refined sugar, salt, once regarded as "white gold," has been converted in modern times to a "white poison." Life is not possible without salt, but our consumption of salt is killing us because table salt is mainly sodium chloride. Natural sea salt consists not only of sodium and chloride but also of all natural elements.

According to *Water and Salt: The Essence of Life* by Dr. Barbara Hendel and biophysicist Peter Ferreira, natural sea salt rebalances the entire body.[21] Sea salt is most effective in stabilizing irregular heartbeats, and, contrary to the misconception that it causes high blood pressure, it is actually essential for the regulation of blood pressure—in conjunction with water. Of course the proportions are critical.

Salt is a strong natural antihistamine and essential for the prevention of muscle cramps.

Note: if you suffer from hypertension, substitute other seasonings instead such as vinegar, garlic, and other fresh herbs.

Sea salt:

▶ Helps extract excess acidity from the cells in the body, particularly the brain cells

▶ Helps generate hydroelectric energy in cells of the body. It is used for local power generation at the sites where energy is needed.

▶ Aids in the absorption of food particles through the intestinal tract

▶ Clears the lungs of mucous plugs and sticky phlegm, particularly in asthma and cystic fibrosis

life-extender tip

Rebalance your entire body with sea salt! Add sea salt to your favorite dishes! Replace table salt with sea salt.

16

Why is olive oil so beneficial?

A prime component of the Mediterranean Diet, olive oil is a natural "juice" that preserves the taste, aroma, vitamins, and properties of the olive fruit. Olive oil is the only vegetable oil that can be consumed as it is freshly pressed from the fruit. The beneficial health effects of olive oil are due to its high content of both anti-oxidants and monounsaturated fatty acids. Studies have shown that olive oil offers protection against heart disease by controlling LDL (bad cholesterol) levels while raising HDL (good cholesterol) levels.

answer

The stomach tolerates olive oil very well.[22] In fact, olive oil has a soothing effect on ulcers and gastritis. Consequently, it lowers the incidence of gallstones.

Spanish researchers suggest that including olive oil in your diet may also offer benefits in terms of colon cancer prevention. Their study results showed rats that were fed a diet supplemented with olive oil had a lower risk of colon cancer than those fed a diet supplemented with safflower oil. In fact, the rats that received olive oil had colon cancer rates almost as low as those fed fish oil, which several studies have already linked to a reduction in risk for colon cancer.

Remember, the less olive oil is handled, the closer it is to its original, most health-boosting state. Extra virgin should be your olive oil of choice.

Store your olive oil in a cool place away from heat and light, and make sure it is tightly sealed. Olive oil is like any other oil: it goes rancid once it has been exposed to air, light, or high temperatures.

Adding this ancient health-promoting oil to your diet offers protection to your heart and flavor to your life!

Olive oil is extracted by pressing or crushing olives multiple times. The earlier the pressing, the higher the quality and nutritional value.

Use these forms of olive oil in your cooking:

▶ Extra virgin—considered the best. It is the least processed and has the highest nutritional value. It is from the first pressing of the olives. Use in salads, salad dressings, and vinaigrettes, or drizzle over crusty bread, brush on fish or meat before serving, or on your baked potato instead of butter. It is not to be used in cooking, frying, or sautéing, because heat alters its chemical composition.

▶ Virgin—from the second pressing. Use this in combination with another oil such as canola, butter, or pure olive oil to cook, fry, or sauté.

▶ Pure—undergoes some processing, filtering, and refining. This is best to use when frying or sautéing because it has a higher smoke point.

▶ Extra light—undergoes considerable processing, only retains a mild olive flavor, could possibly contain other oils, and has the least health benefits

life-extender tip

Use olive oil in cooking and in salads! Your heart will thank you!

question

17 What spices pack the most health-building punch?

Spices have been used not only for their pungent flavors and the excitement they add to cuisine, but also for their health-promoting benefits as well. For centuries, cultures in India, Greece, Italy, Jamaica, the Virgin Islands, the Caribbean, South America, and Asia have incorporated spices in their everyday cooking, making their dishes savory, their health robust, and their tastes enviable the world over.

answer

Here is a list of just a few of the many spices and the ways they are used so that you can take advantage of their most powerful healing and preventative agents.

Cayenne

Cayenne contains capsaicin, a compound proven to block substance P, the brain chemical involved in the transmission of pain impulses. Capsaicin also boosts the body's production of natural painkillers called endorphins. In addition, capsaicin destroys the ulcer-causing bacterium *heliobacter pylori*.

How to use it: For pain relief, soak a gauze pad in a hot pepper sauce containing cayenne and apply it to your painful area. For ulcers and blocked airway passages, simply add 1/2 teaspoon of hot pepper sauce or cayenne to hot water and lemon and drink.

Rosemary

Rosemary prevents the breakdown of acetylcholine, a neurotransmitter that is deficient in patients with Alzheimer's disease. Eating rosemary may reduce your risk of developing Alzheimer's.

How to use it: Add rosemary to your recipes, when possible, like chicken, fish, and potatoes.

Garlic

One of nature's most potent antibiotics, garlic inhibits the growth of fungi, yeast, and bacteria, including strains that are becoming resistant to synthetic antibiotics. Garlic also contains allicin, a compound that works like aspirin to thin the blood, and it helps prevent atherosclerosis.

How to use it: Cook with it, and your heart will thank you!

Ginger

Highly prized in Asia as medicine and part of their daily life, ginger is safe and effective and has served as a home remedy for billions of people when it comes to stomach upset, poor circulation, and the common cold. While fresh ginger is very potent, both powdered and fresh ginger are wonderful in cooking.

How to use it: For the common cold, drink two cups of ginger tea or take two 500 mg capsules.

Spices will:

▶ Boost the body's production of endorphins
▶ Reduce your risk of developing Alzheimer's and atherosclerosis
▶ Inhibit growth of fungi, yeast, and bacteria
▶ Calm the stomach and speed digestion

life-extender tip

Start using and cooking with these healthy spices today.

question

18

Is there a supplement I can take to help boost my recall?

Just like omega-3 fatty acids, phospholipids are also important for optimal brain health. As the name implies, phospholipids are made of the combination of lipids (fats) and the mineral phosphorus. Phospholipids are found in high concentrations in the lining of practically every cell of the body, including brain cells. They help brain cells communicate and influence how well receptors function. Although present in many foods, phospholipids are found in higher concentrations in soy, eggs, and the brain tissue of animals. One of the most common phospholipids is phosphatidyl serene or PS.

answer

A well-documented nutrient used in Europe to reverse age-related memory loss and dementia is phosphatidyl serene, or PS for short.[23] It is a compound that is made naturally by the body and has the ability to lower your stress response. PS is a brain-cell nutrient that rapidly crosses the blood brain barrier. PS boosts neurotransmitters in your brain that activate concentration, reasoning, and memory. This translates into your body having more ability to withstand the harmful effects of stress.

Often these benefits will persist for weeks after PS is stopped. Common foods have insignificant amounts of PS, and the body produces limited amounts.

When taking PS, be patient. As with many natural supplements, it may take up to three months before you notice a measurable difference!

In addition to adding PS to your life-extending plan, there are additional steps you can take to improve your memory. In many cases, memory problems associated with aging are simply related to mental inactivity and/or stress.

Physical activity is also a memory booster. Aerobic exercise boosts circulation throughout your body, and that includes your brain! Increased flow to the brain has been shown to increase mental function.

Another way to increase blood flow to the brain is to eat a low-fat diet. The arteries that feed the brain are tiny, so any narrowing that occurs at all can make a difference. Eating fatty or cholesterol-rich foods can narrow these small arteries and reduce oxygen flow. Tiny strokes are related to blood flow problems in the brain and may be related to age-related memory loss.

Additional supplements to protect the brain from age-related memory loss are gingko biloba, antioxidants (selenium and vitamins C and E), and acetyl L-carnitine.

Other brain-boosting activities include doing crossword puzzles, playing chess, Sudoku, or keeping a daily journal.

Improve your memory by:

▶ Adding a PS supplement to your life-extending plan

▶ Getting aerobic exercise to boost circulation

▶ Eating a low-fat diet

▶ Taking other beneficial supplements, including gingko biloba, antioxidants (selenium and vitamins C and E), and acetyl L-carnitine

life-extender tip

Boost your brainpower! Take 200–300 mg of phosphatidyl serene (PS) daily.

19 Is there a supplement that can help rev up my metabolism?

The speed at which our metabolism functions is influenced by many factors: age, gender, heredity, and proportion of lean body mass. The older we get, the slower our metabolism functions. After age forty, the metabolism slows 5 percent per decade. Metabolism establishes the rate at which we burn calories and how efficiently the body uses the fuel it is fed through food. Hormones and enzymes are what convert food into fuel, and there are ways to supplement the hormones and enzymes you need to boost your sluggish metabolism.[24]

answer

Acetyl L-carnitine and carnitine play several important roles in the human body, particularly energizing the metabolism. They are widely available in animal foods and dairy products, but plant-based foods have very small amounts. When taken as a pill, carnitine is not able to cross the blood brain barrier as well as its activated form acetyl L-carnitine. ALC has significantly more noticeable effects than carnitine alone.

An amino acid manufactured in your liver, ALC helps facilitate fat metabolism, increases energy production in muscle cells, promotes fat loss, and increases circulation in the brain. In other words, the body uses ALC to turn fat into energy—a very good thing! It is also a natural antioxidant and is thought to have specific benefit to the brain, particularly for decreasing the effects of Alzheimer's disease and age-related cognitive decline.

In the world of medicine, ALC is primarily used to treat heart-related problems. Some studies suggest that ALC may be useful in helping individuals suffering from adult-onset diabetes to better control their blood sugar levels.

ALC has been tested in the therapy of depression and shown to be helpful in improving mood. Out of sixty subjects, aged sixty to eighty years, with low mood, half were given 3 grams a day of ALC while the other half received a placebo.[25] The results showed that treatment with ALC induced a significant reduction in the severity of depressive symptoms and also a significant improvement in the quality of life.

ALC is available in doses ranging between 100 and 500 mg. Carnitine is useful for fighting fatigue and is available in a variety of doses ranging from 250 to 750 mg and is also sold as a powder.

ALC has far-reaching benefits. Rev up your metabolism and your cerebral function today with ALC and carnitine!

Acetyl L-carnitine:

- ▶ Is known to help supply the brain with energy to function at its best and has a positive impact on memory, mood, and cognitive ability
- ▶ Occurs naturally in most meats and dairy products and may be taken as a dietary supplement
- ▶ May improve the energy production of the body and has sparked the curiosity of those who study everything from muscle diseases to heart disorders

life-extender tip

Add to your diet today acetyl L-carnitine or carnitine in capsule form or powder.

20 What can I do to keep my blood sugar from crashing?

Chromium helps to keep blood sugar in balance, metabolizes amino acids and fats, and helps to lower bad cholesterol while raising the good! Elevated blood sugar spurs the body to secrete insulin, and chronically high insulin levels can lead to obesity, high blood pressure, and high triglycerides. All of these reactions boost your risk of heart disease! As we get older, our bodies store less of this wonderful mineral, which may account for the reason age is one of the biggest risk factors in the development of diabetes. Therefore, chromium is very useful for controlling diabetes and hypoglycemia as well as preventing cardiovascular disease.

answer

Tests show that people with diabetes have lower levels of chromium circulating in their blood than people without the disease. In one study, eight people who had difficulty regulating blood sugar were given 200 mcg of chromium a day. After five weeks, their blood sugar levels fell by as much as 50 percent. People without blood sugar problems who were given chromium showed no such changes.[26] So in essence, chromium offers you "chrome-plated" protection.

Chromium, found in broccoli, grapefruit, and fortified breakfast cereals, has been shown to help regulate blood sugar, according to Richard A. Anderson, PhD, a research chemist with the USDA Human Nutrition Research Council in Beltsville, Maryland.[27] Chromium supplements help especially if you are chromium deficient. Richard Anderson says that studies show that about 90 percent of diabetics and the general population do not get enough chromium in their diets. Virtually all adults, says Anderson, could benefit from taking 50–200 mcg daily.[28]

Chromium is a difficult mineral to absorb, and most of it is eliminated through the kidneys and bowels. To help your body retain the most chromium, it's wise to eat lots of complex carbohydrates, like pasta and bagels. Eating sugary foods, on the other hand, will cause your body to excrete chromium.

With this in mind, you should take steps to add chromium picolinate supplements or chromium-rich foods to your diet today. Other food sources include beets, nuts, black pepper, mushrooms, broccoli, brewer's yeast, barley, and blackstrap molasses.

Chromium helps:

▶ Stabilize blood sugar levels and make your energy consistent

▶ Metabolize amino acids and fats, thus helping control your weight

▶ Lower bad cholesterol while raising the good

life-extender tip

Take 200 mcg of chromium picolinate daily if you are 150 pounds or less. If you weigh over 150 pounds, 400 mcg is recommended.

Royal jelly has been used for centuries by civilizations around the world to treat and combat the onset of countless ailments and medical conditions. This thick, milky substance is secreted from the pharyngeal glands of a special group of young nurse bees between their sixth and twelfth day of life. It is the sole food for the queen bee, who grows 50 percent larger and lives forty times longer than other bees.

answer

Royal jelly is a powerful antioxidant. It increases digestion; aids women in their menopausal years by nourishing the adrenal glands; fights bacteria; improves the beauty of hair, skin, and nails; helps to prevent atherosclerosis; and significantly lowers cholesterol and triglyceride levels.

Royal jelly is a rich source of proteins, fatty acids, sugars, sterols, and phosphorous compounds and acetylcholine, which transmits nerve messages from cell to cell. In addition, this royal substance contains gamma globulin, which is known to stimulate the immune system and fight off infections.

Royal jelly supplies all B vitamins; vitamins A, C, D, E, and K; more than a dozen key minerals; eighteen amino acids; and nucleic acids DNA and RNA.

Packed with all of these vitamins, minerals, and essential amino acids, royal jelly can provide you with essential nutrition for your fast-paced life!

According to Rita Elkins, MH, in her book *Bee Pollen, Royal Jelly, Propolis and Honey*, royal jelly:[29]

▶ Slows aging and promotes longevity
▶ Stimulates the immune system and fights infection
▶ Regulates and balances hormones
▶ Increases vigor and physical strength
▶ Can help to regulate weight
▶ Stimulates memory and mental function
▶ Fights chronic fatigue
▶ Helps with stress and anxiety
▶ Boosts endocrine and adrenal gland health
▶ Helps relieve menopausal symptoms
▶ Contributes to smooth, youthful looking skin

Note: If you are allergic to bee products, pollen, honey, or bee stings, you should avoid royal jelly. Instead, go for a different "bee." Take a B-complex vitamin!

Here's the buzz straight from the hive—royal jelly:

▶ Is a powerful antioxidant
▶ Increases digestion
▶ Aids menopausal women by nourishing adrenal glands
▶ Fights bacteria
▶ Improves the beauty of hair, skin, and nails
▶ Helps prevent atherosclerosis and significantly lowers cholesterol and triglyceride levels

life-extender tip

Taking 500–1,000 mg of royal jelly (capsule or liquid) can add life to your years!

22 How and why do we need to protect our DNA?

The simple process of aging depletes your storehouse of nucleic acids, which are the building blocks of your DNA and RNA. Each cell of your body contains DNA and RNA. Exposure to chemicals, harsh environmental factors, and lower levels of protective phytonutrients in the diet make it important to support healthy function of DNA in our bodies. Proper function of our DNA code, imprinted in all nucleated cells of our body, and proper function of our immune system may well be the two most critical factors involved in maintaining health. The major function of DNA, beyond carrying the genetic traits of our ancestors, is to duplicate itself exactly when cells divide.

answer

It is crucial to protect DNA in order to continually synthesize perfect copies of complex proteins called enzymes in order to maintain healthy metabolism and cellular functions.[30]

DNA maintenance enzymes within the cells are responsible for ensuring that the code remains the same when a cell divides, accomplishing this before, during, or after cell division. Your body ensures cellular health through a process called apoptosis. During apoptosis, cells that are unable to maintain accurate DNA copies through their own DNA repair mechanisms are broken down and recycled. The body has numerous such processes to maintain and promote healthy DNA, which results in healthy cells, including a healthy immune system.

To protect and promote healthy DNA, it is important to know that vitamin B_{12} and folic acid play a role in methylation reactions, which are essential to maintaining healthy DNA. In addition, vitamins B_{12}, B_9 (folic acid), B_8 (biotin), and B_6 (pyridoxine) promote cell longevity, DNA and RNA production, nucleic acid formation, and RNA/DNA action.

Rich food sources of nucleic acids include mushrooms, spinach, asparagus, salmon, and wheat germ.

While you cannot halt the aging process, you can try to slow it down and make living a more healthful, joyful experience.

Protecting DNA keeps aging at bay!

Replenishing your stock of nucleic acids may:

▶ Slow down the aging process

▶ Increase energy

▶ Promote healthier skin and reduce age spots

life-extender tip

Add nucleic-rich foods to your diet today such as salmon, mushrooms, wheat germ, asparagus, and spinach! Or you may add a B-complex vitamin to your longevity regimen.

23 Can gingko help me keep my memory sharp as I grow older?

Ginkgo trees are the oldest living trees on earth. The tree has long been utilized to support a long and healthy life. For centuries, Chinese and Japanese traditions have used gingko leaves to support the brain, heart, and lungs. The active components of gingko biloba, ginkgoheterosides and terpene lactones, enhance the flow of oxygen and blood to the brain and promote transmission of nerve impulses, supporting mental acuity. Gingko biloba offers nutritional support to the vascular system by sustaining the strength and elasticity of blood vessels and capillaries. In addition, it maintains healthy platelet function and acts as a free-radical scavenger.

answer

One of *the* most studied plants, gingko has been confirmed to boost circulation to the brain and other organs, improving memory and cognitive functions. In addition, gingko has been used widely as a longevity tonic in Asia and Europe. The leaf of the gingko is even shaped like a human brain!

Gingko leaves were mentioned in a major Chinese herbal text of the Ming Dynasty in 1436 and another in 1505. A standardized extract was developed in the past twenty years in Germany for the treatment of cerebral dysfunction, which includes dizziness, tinnitus, headaches, emotional instability with anxiety, and difficulty in memory. It is also licensed as a supportive treatment for hearing loss due to cervical syndrome and for peripheral arterial circulatory disturbances, such as intermittent claudication (a severe pain in the calf muscles resulting from inadequate blood supply).[31]

At least three volumes of technical papers on the chemistry, pharmacology, and clinical studies on gingko biloba have been published.[32] This only goes to further prove that adding gingko to your antiaging arsenal will give you a time-tested, nutritional way to support circulation and mental acuity.[33]

Gingko biloba:

▶ Enhances the flow of oxygen and blood to the brain and promotes transmission of nerve impulses, supporting mental acuity

▶ Supports the vascular system by sustaining the strength and elasticity of blood vessels and capillaries

▶ Maintains healthy platelet function and acts as a free-radical scavenger

▼ life-extender tip

Add 160 mg of gingko two times daily to your life for mental sharpness and blood flow.

24

How do we keep our foods relatively pesticide free?

In today's world, we are bombarded with many toxins that can over time damage our health—including the pesticides used in agriculture to protect crops from insect damage and infestation. It is imperative that you become proactive when it comes to limiting your exposure to these toxins on a daily basis because it is now known that they have a cumulative effect that can contribute to diseases such as cancer.

answer

Produce with the lowest amounts of pesticide residue are the hard-skinned fruits and vegetables like squash, pineapples, corn, citrus, melons, and avocados. Foods with the highest residue levels include some items that can be peeled—zucchini, cucumbers, peaches, and plums.

The following are best eaten when organic—grapes, cherries, celery, strawberries, and tomatoes.

Also, you should know that pesticide sprays used in homes to kill ants, roaches, and more are made up of chemicals that can shorten your life span. Researchers have found that children living in households that use pesticides have a much higher risk of developing childhood leukemia. You should choose today's new "chemical-free" pest controllers that are available at most health food stores.

Here's more. Chlordane, a pesticide composed of over fifty different chemicals and that mimics estrogen, was banned in the United States over fifty years ago. But it has continued to be manufactured in the States and shipped to Mexico, where it was sprayed on food crops exported back to the States! According to the Agency for Toxic Substances and Disease Registry, almost every human on earth has chlordane in their fat. There is no way to get it out of the body. Losing weight only concentrates the chemical in the remaining fat. Besides being sprayed on America's corn, millions of tons of chlordane were put into the ground around house foundations to kill termites before it was banned. The half-life of chlordane in soil is twenty-two years. This means that it will not degrade for at least forty years![34]

The good news here is that curcumin (an herb from India also called turmeric) has been shown to have the ability to block many dangerous chemicals, including chlordane.[35]

Recommendations to reduce the amount of exposure to pesticides:

▶ Wash the foods you are going to eat.

▶ Do not plant near a house foundation that could have been treated with chlordane.

▶ Cook with curcumin or turmeric.

▶ Choose hard-skinned fruits and vegetables like squash, pineapples, corn, citrus, melons, and avocados; peel soft-skinned fruits and vegetables; or eat organic fruits and vegetables.

life-extender tip

Reduce your risk of exposure to harmful pesticides by peeling off the outer layer of your fruits and vegetables. Buy organic produce when possible.

question

25

Why is drinking the right amount of water so important?

Did you know that water is second only to oxygen in importance for health and that just a few short days without water can be fatal? Water makes up almost three-fourths of your body, and every cell is regulated, monitored, and dependent on an efficient flow of water. Water carries minerals, vitamins, proteins, and sugar around your body for assimilation. It maintains your body's temperature and equilibrium; lubricates tissues; flushes wastes and toxins; hydrates your skin; acts as a shock absorber for your joints, bones, and muscles; and adds needed minerals.

answer

Adequate hydration insures that all systems are "go" in terms of your ability to feel vibrant and energized. Conversely, dehydration plays a role in ailments of elimination like constipation, urinary tract infections, peripheral vascular problems like hemorrhoids and varicose veins, kidney stones, and even degenerative diseases like arthritis.

It is important to remember that thirst is not a reliable indicator of dehydration. By the time you feel thirsty, you probably are suffering from some degree of dehydration. Plain or carbonated cool water is the best way to replace body fluids, but other healthy beverages can also count toward replenishment. Choices include vegetable juices and diluted fruit juices. Caffeine and alcohol drinks are diuretics and therefore are not recommended. Drinks that are full of sugars or dairy will increase your body's need for water instead of adding to hydration. Soft drinks leach important minerals from your body and are not recommended.

Many people who are thought to be senile are actually just severely dehydrated! This is due to the disorientation and memory loss that dehydration causes.

It is recommended that you drink eight to ten 8-ounce glasses of water daily. If you are physically active or working in hot summer conditions, you should drink more. I recommend squeezing half a lemon and adding the juice to each glass of water when possible because it boosts water's ability to dilute and eliminate toxins in the bloodstream and kidneys.

Water naturally suppresses your appetite and helps your body metabolize stored fat. If you are dehydrated, fat deposits tend to increase, so the more water you drink—more fat deposits are reduced! So drink up!

It's time to check to see if you are drinking enough water.

You need to drink more water if you have:

▶ Dark yellow urine (the color of your urine should be a pale straw color and you should urinate every few hours)

▶ Unusually dry skin and loss of appetite along with constipation

▶ Unexplained headaches (mild to severe accompanied by dizziness)

▶ Dull back pain that is not relieved by rest

▶ Swollen hands and/or feet

life-extender tip

Drink a glass of water as soon as you wake up to replenish fluids lost during sleep. Have a glass of water before any meal or snack to help control your appetite.

question

Is it true that you can extend your life by walking regularly?

Walking is safe and burns almost as many calories as jogging. It is probably *the* safest exercise you can do! It does not require expensive training, special equipment, instructional videos, computer programs, or special manuals. It doesn't require prior training or conditioning, and it doesn't require a great deal of physical exertion in the beginning. Studies have even shown that due to the grand design of your body, walking is more natural than sitting, standing, or running, and walking is not as stressful to the body as other forms of exercise.[36] Walking eases back pains, slims your waist, lowers blood pressure, reduces levels of bad cholesterol, reduces heart attack risk, enhances stamina and energy, lessens anxiety and tension, improves muscle tone, is easy on your joints, reduces your appetite, increases aerobic capacity, can be done in short bouts, slows down osteoporosis and bone loss, and can be done even when traveling!

answer

If you want to live healthier and longer, start with daily walking or exercise. A study in the November 14, 2005, *Archives of Internal Medicine* found that exercise levels were directly related to years lived without cardiovascular disease. A moderate level of physical activity, such as walking thirty minutes a day, lengthened life by 1.3 years and added 1.1 more years without cardiovascular disease, compared with those with low activity levels. People in the study who chose a high activity level gained 3.7 years of life and added 3.3 more years without cardiovascular disease.[37]

Let's do the math: If you invest thirty minutes of walking a day, you'll spend forty-nine days of the next twelve years of your life walking to gain 1.3 healthy years. That's a pretty good return on your health investment, especially since walking will help you lose weight and improve your mood too!

Walking 101—a few
tips to get you started:

► Posture is key. In order to get the most benefit from your walking program, good posture is critical. Keep your head up, your spine straight, and look straight ahead. Keep your arms and shoulders loose.

► Breathe! Take regular deep breaths. Never hold your breath.

► Walk—don't run! To get the most out of your walk, you should keep a brisk pace but not fast.

► Try to take long, smooth strides. Your motion should be effortless with your arms swinging at your sides for balance.

► Pay attention to what your body is telling you. If you have any pain or discomfort, check with your doctor.

life-extender tip

Walking thirty minutes a day can add years to your life! It was Hippocrates who said, "Walking is man's best medicine." Now…thousands of years later, we are still discovering new benefits daily.

question

27 Is it true that exercise can help prevent mental decline?

Most of us know that physical exercise is good for our general health, but did you know that physical exercise is also good for your brain? If you think you're going to get smarter sitting in front of your computer or watching television, think again.

answer

When it comes to aging, physical exercise has a protective effect on the brain and its mental processes, and it may even help prevent Alzheimer's disease. Based on exercise and health data from nearly five thousand men and women over sixty-five years of age, those who exercised were less likely to lose their mental abilities or develop dementia, including Alzheimer's. Furthermore, the more a person exercises, the greater the protective benefits for the brain, particularly in women. Inactive individuals in a recent study were twice as likely to develop Alzheimer's, compared to those with the highest levels of activity (exercised vigorously at least three times a week). But even light or moderate exercisers cut their risk significantly for Alzheimer's and mental decline.[38]

If you have reached middle age, or passed it, and have never have exercised regularly, the good news is that it is not too late to start. Physical activity improves mental function by inducing the growth of capillaries, which are tiny blood vessels in the brain. Capillaries help nutrients reach neurons. This is very important because the aging process leads to a decrease in blood supply to the brain.

For decades, it has been considered a scientific fact that the brains of adult mammals had a fixed number of cells. This idea has been challenged recently by several studies that showed exercise nearly doubled the number of cells in the area of the brain involved with learning and memory, known as the hippocampus. This study was done on mice, but regeneration of the hippocampus has now been shown in adult birds and monkeys. One researcher speculated "intense exercise in a natural environment may be associated with a need for increased navigation skills." The hippocampus is thought to be the control center for the learning processes involved with navigating and understanding our surroundings.[39]

Physical exercise also leads to deep, recuperative sleep. It is during this deep sleep state that your brain gets the opportunity to consolidate memory and rebalance hormones and brain chemicals to get you ready for a new day! Every step you take to improve your physical well-being will positively influence your brain health. Exercise is good not only for your body but for your mind as well!

Mind enhancement is a lifelong process. Add exercise to your protocol for a long-lasting brain!

Regular physical exercise:

▶ Increases brain cells
▶ Reduces the risk of Alzheimer's and dementia
▶ Improves sleep
▶ Strengthens memory
▶ Helps keep hormones in balance

life-extender tip

Take a thirty-minute walk each day to live healthier and longer.

question

28 Is it true that soft drinks can contribute to osteoporosis?

Preventing osteoporosis is a lifelong endeavor. Nicotine, caffeine, and excessive sugar and salt play a role in weakening the calcium in your bones. In other words, they are "bad to the bone." Caffeinated cola soft drinks are one of the biggest offenders because they are high in phosphorus, which can leach calcium from our bones. But simply avoiding soft drinks and other caffeinated beverages may not be enough.

answer

Researchers at Tufts University, studying several thousand men and women, found that women who regularly drank cola-based sodas—three or more a day—had almost 4 percent lower bone mineral density in the hip, even though researchers controlled for calcium and vitamin D intake. Here are the details of the study to really drive the point home to you.

Researchers examined dietary intake and hip and spine bone mineral density in more than twenty-five hundred men and women in their fifties and sixties. After adjusting for body mass index, height, age, energy intake, physical activity level, smoking, menopausal status and estrogen use (in women only), and intake of alcohol, caffeine, vitamin D, and calcium, they found that cola intake in women was associated with significantly lower bone mineral density of the hip. Drinking one daily serving of cola decreased a woman's bone density by 4–5 percent, while consuming noncola carbonated beverages had no effect on bone density.[40]

Another study reported on Healthy.net also confirmed that the daily consumption of cola beverages is associated with decreased bone mineral density in older women.[41]

To help keep your bones healthy, you should select from the following beverages:

▶ Mineral or distilled water
▶ Herbal or green tea
▶ Soy or rice milk instead of cow's milk
▶ Coffee and tea in limited amounts (they are acidic, even if decaffeinated)
▶ Alcohol—less than 5 ounces per week

Women tend to lose 1 to 3 percent of their bone mass yearly during the first five to ten years after entering menopause. So get your bones tested. You should have a "baseline" test to determine if you have lost any bone density. A bone mineral density test (BMD) measures the amount of mineral in your bones. It can identify how strong your bones currently are and provide a baseline for determining whether a bone-strengthening program is indicated.

I recommend that every woman have a BMD test during perimenopause or during the first year after menstruation has ceased.

To help prevent bone loss:

▶ Avoid cola-based sodas
▶ Drink soy or rice milk and calcium-fortified orange juice
▶ Avoid caffeine, nicotine, and excessive salt and sugar

life-extender tip

For every soda you skip, drink a glass of milk or calcium-fortified orange juice instead. I like to add fruit juice to sparkling water for a "healthy soda" that contains health-boosting antioxidants along with the sparkling fizz that refreshes!

29

Can vitamin D help prevent bone loss?

Have you ever wondered why women who take calcium supplements still suffer from a loss of bone mineral density? One reason is that most women do not take enough elemental calcium to offset the amount being lost in the course of normal aging. Bone density loss is not just associated with calcium deficiency, but a host of other nutrient deficiencies, especially vitamin D_3.

answer

Known as the "silent epidemic," vitamin D deficiency affects 54 percent of all homebound elderly men and women and 21–58 percent of adolescents and adults in the United States.[42]

You may unknowingly be one of these millions of Americans whose body is plagued by the lack of this one essential substance. The lack of vitamin D is associated with a host of age-related problems such as cancer, cardiovascular disease, multiple sclerosis, rheumatoid arthritis, and type 1 diabetes mellitus in adults.[43]

Vitamin D_3 is synthesized in the skin in response to sunlight exposure, but few people achieve optimal levels this way, due in part to the limited ultraviolet light available during winter months. This seasonal deficit is compounded by the fact that many people are now avoiding sun exposure during spring and summer months because of concern about premature skin aging and cancers like melanoma. Alarming new research suggests that these factors are contributing to a year-round epidemic of vitamin D deficiency, particularly in elderly adults.

Many published studies show that low calcium intake is associated with low bone mass, rapid bone loss, and high fracture rates. Vitamin D_3 plays an important role in calcium absorption and bone health. It is made in the skin after exposure to sunlight, but it can also be obtained through the diet. Individuals who consume adequate amounts of calcium and vitamin D_3 throughout life are more likely to achieve optimal skeletal mass early in life and are less likely to lose bone later in life.

Vitamin D_3 does far more than promote healthy teeth and bones. As I mentioned, its role in supporting immunity, modulating inflammation, and preventing cancer makes the consequences of vitamin D_3 deficiency potentially devastating. A growing number of scientists who study vitamin D levels in human populations now recommend annual blood tests to check vitamin D status.

As you age, changes in your skin's structure will reduce your ability to convert vitamin D to its active form by up to 60 percent by the time you reach age sixty-five.[44]

Taking sufficient vitamin D_3:

▶ Promotes healthy teeth and bones
▶ Supports immunity
▶ Modulates inflammation
▶ Helps prevent cancer
▶ Promotes calcium absorption

life-extender tip

Regular outdoor activities strengthen your bones and expose you to the sunlight your body needs to create vitamin D for calcium absorption. Suggested dose: 1,000 mg vitamin D_3 daily.

question

30
What benefits does ginseng provide?

Ginseng is known as a plant-derived adaptogen, which simply means that it helps us "adapt" to the mental and physical rigors of our modern lifestyles. It is important to note that ginseng is the name given to three different plants. The most widely known is Panax ginseng, also known as Korean, Chinese, or Asian ginseng. Animal studies have shown that bioactive compounds in ginseng improve the sensitivity of the HPA, or the hypothalamic-pituitary-adrenal axis, to cortisol. HPA axis is the interaction between the hypothalamus, the pituitary gland, and the adrenal or suprarenal glands; it also helps regulate your temperature, digestion, immune system, mood, sexuality, and energy usage and is a major part of the system that controls your reaction to stress, trauma, and injury.[45] This means that ginseng provides protection against both physical and psychological stresses.

answer

Ginseng has been widely studied for its relationship to the process of aging among humans. A study on the direct effects of ginsenoside Rg1, extracted from Panax ginseng, on lymphocytes of aged people was conducted by scientists at the Beijing Institute of Geriatrics. The scientists found that the Rg1 saponin used could "stimulate and enhance the function of lymphocytes, restoring it to normal. Furthermore," the report details, "this study provided insight on the benefits of saponin and other herbs. Ginseng contains ten saponins (polysaccharides) with specific characteristics, including Rc, Rc2, Rd, and Rg1. Some of the researchers found that ginseng can promote synthesis of protein, RNA, and DNA in tissues and organs such as the kidney, liver, bone marrow, and plasma."[46]

Ginseng has a wide range of therapeutic uses. The main application is with stressed, weak, or debilitated persons, but all of its far-reaching benefits can be especially useful. In addition, ginseng may help to reduce cholesterol and stimulate the immune system and endocrine responses.[47]

Control stress and boost your antiaging arsenal with:

▶ Aerobic exercise for thirty minutes three to five times a week

▶ Stress-management techniques such as relaxation, meditation, and prayer

▶ Ginseng and other nutritional supplements

life-extender tip

Add zing to your life with ginseng, 100–300 mg daily. Ginseng tea, capsules, or extract can be a potent source of energy. Be sure not to mix ginseng with caffeine or another stimulant. The combination could cause palpitations.

31 Is stevia a good alternative to artificial sweeteners?

Humans have long been looking for ways to satisfy sweet cravings. In ancient days, honey satisfied our sweet desires. Later, mankind learned all about the new kid on the block—sugar cane and other crops that could also sweeten our lives. But that was then, when we lived more physically active lives with jobs that were more physically demanding and when sugar was not abused but rather enjoyed and appreciated as an occasional indulgence. Wow, have things changed! Now, many of us have sedentary jobs and lifestyles, and we can get foods from the nearest refrigerator, fast-food restaurant, vending machine, or convenience store. Along with these modern culinary conveniences are calorie-free sweeteners to satisfy our industrialized sweet tooth.

answer

Aspartame, cyclamate, saccharin, and acesulfame-K are chemicals used as artificial sweeteners. Research has shown that they stimulate the urge to overeat. Aspartame and saccharin have been associated with mental and emotional problems. Cyclamate has unresolved questions concerning its association with cancer. In 1969, the FDA banned the use of cyclamate due to concerns that it could raise the risk of bladder cancer.[48] As of 2007, the FDA was reviewing a petition to reapprove the substance. Sucralose is a chemical made by modifying sugar. It is six hundred times sweeter than table sugar. Nevertheless, it is not a food, and like any other drug or chemical, it may have side effects and may not be eliminated from your body.

In an interesting "landmark study of more than 80,000 nurses, Harvard researchers found that the single best dietary predictor of weight gain was how much saccharin the women ate."[49] In the book *The Doctors Book of Food Remedies*, Selene Yeager revealed that people who used artificial sweeteners were, on average, two pounds heavier than people who did not![50] Even though artificial sweeteners add little or no calories, they will only help you lose weight as you decide to use them *instead* of sugar. Since artificial sweeteners arrived on the market, consumption of both regular sugar and artificial sugars has gone up. We have just added them to our sugar consumption, so we are getting more total calories.

If you need to sweeten your food, an excellent natural herbal alternative to both sugar and artificial sweeteners is stevia. Stevia, which is thirty times sweeter than sugar but contains no calories, has been used as a sweetener in Paraguay for over fifteen hundred years and surrounding countries for centuries. Stevia is a wonderful weight-loss aid because it contains no calories; research indicates it significantly increases glucose absorption. Use it to sweeten your teas, coffee, and favorite recipes! The good news is—look, Ma—no chemicals!

Artificial sweeteners:

▶ Stimulate overeating
▶ Have dangerous side effects
▶ Increase sugar consumption
▶ Are inferior to healthy, natural stevia

life-extender tip

Try to avoid all artificial sweeteners. Use a natural sweetener such as stevia instead.

question

32 How do I avoid dangerous food additives?

Processed foods contain many unwanted additives that can cause cell degeneration and are a significant contributor to the aging process. There are over fourteen thousand man-made food additives in our American food supply today. While a little of these additives may be considered "harmless," think about total daily, weekly, and yearly consumption. Our bodies were not designed to process these substances. Avoid them whenever possible—or at least limit your intake!

answer

Acesulfame-K is a sugar substitute sold in packet form. It is the sweetening ingredient in chewing gum, certain beverages, dry mixes for beverages, instant coffee, tea, gelatin desserts, puddings, and nondairy creamers. Studies have shown that it causes cancer in animals, and it may increase cancer in humans as well.[51]

BHA and BHT—these two closely related chemicals are added to oil-containing foods to prevent oxidation and rancidity. The chemical has been found in three species of animals. Therefore the U.S. Department of Health and Human Services considers BHA to be possibly carcinogenic to humans. Some studies show that BHT may also increase the risk of cancer.[52]

MSG (monosodium glutamate)—the substance in certain seasonings (especially Asian) that adds flavor to protein-containing foods. Consuming too much MSG has been linked to tightness in the chest, headaches, and burning sensations in the body.

Olestra—despite being approved by the FDA, all snacks containing olestra must carry a warning label that states: "This product contains olestra. Olestra may cause abdominal cramping and loose stools. Olestra inhibits the absorption of some vitamins and other nutrients. Vitamins A, D, E, and K have been added."

Nitrate and nitrite—these two chemicals are closely related and are used to preserve meat. Nitrate itself is harmless, but it is readily converted to nitrites or nitrosamines, which are extremely powerful cancer-causing chemicals during the cooking process such as frying or grilling.[53] Nitrites are a possible contributor to stomach cancer. Look for nitrate-free meats! Hot dogs and bacon are the worst offenders!

Potassium bromate—rarely used in California because a cancer warning is required on the label—has been used to increase the volume of bread to produce bread with a fine crumb texture. Bromate has been banned virtually world-wide except for in the United States and Japan.[54]

Sulfites help to keep cut fruits and veggies looking fresh, but studies now show that they can and do provoke sometimes severe allergic responses.[55]

Read food labels and try to avoid:

▶ Acesulfame-K
▶ BHA and BHT
▶ MSG (monosodium glutamate)
▶ Olestra
▶ Nitrates and nitrites
▶ Potassium bromate
▶ Sulfites

life-extender tip

Additives in your foods can accelerate the aging process, so know which ones to avoid, read food labels, and limit your intake of food products that contain them.

33
What soup should I eat to detoxify my body and lose weight?

Soup is a great way to sneak high-nutrient, high-fiber foods into your meals. Eating homemade nutritious soup that is low in salt will not only nourish you but will also flush waste from your body. This simple dietary change may cut your risk of premature death from heart disease, stroke, cancer, etc. Adding soup to the beginning of your meals not only boosts your nutrition, but it also curbs your appetite.

answer

The key is to stick to a serving of low-calorie, high-fiber soup like vegetable soup or minestrone, which only has around 75 to 125 calories. For optimal nutrition and weight loss, try eating at least two homemade "soup meals" a day. And for the best results, try my favorite health-building Slimming Soup!

To get you started, I have included one of my all-time favorite vegetable-based, high-fiber soups that will fill you up—not out!

Dr. Janet's Very Veggie Slimming Soup

2 Tbsp. olive oil
1 large onion, chopped
2 green and/or red bell peppers, chopped
4 garlic cloves, minced
½ tsp. ground cumin
½ small head cabbage, sliced
2 large carrots, sliced
1 zucchini, chopped

1 yellow squash, chopped
1 can (14 ½ oz.) low-sodium stewed tomatoes
1 bottle (46 oz.) vegetable juice
½ tsp. ground black pepper
¼ tsp. crushed red pepper flakes

Warm oil in a large saucepan over medium heat. Add onion and bell peppers. Cook five minutes or until tender. Add garlic and cumin. Cook one minute. Add cabbage, carrots, zucchini, squash, tomatoes (with juice), vegetable juice, black pepper, and red pepper flakes. Heat to boiling. Reduce heat to low, cover, and simmer one hour.

Makes six wonderful servings! It will be easy for you to get your five servings of vegetables today with this soup, and that is just "souper"!

Good, healthy soups will:

▶ Detoxify your body

▶ Increase your vitamin and mineral intake

▶ Add much-needed fiber to your diet

▶ Help you manage your weight

life-extender tip

For optimum health and weight loss, try eating two "soup meals" a day.

As baby boomers age, doctors are seeing more middle-aged people with hearing loss. Hearing loss is the third most common health problem for people over sixty-five. For men, it starts much earlier than that. The National Institute on Aging says that men start losing their hearing in their twenties, while women do not have noticeable hearing loss until their sixties. Most hearing loss cases are noise induced. Years of exposure to loud concerts, cranked-up stereos, personal CD players, leaf blowers, and other environmental noise are a big part of the reason why. It used to be that people aged sixty-five and older were most likely to need hearing aids, but now according to the American Speech-Language-Hearing Association (ASHA), 14 percent of adults between forty-five and sixty-four have hearing loss.[56] But there is hope!

answer

A Dutch study of men and women aged fifty to seventy shows that folic acid—a B vitamin also known as folate—may slow age-related hearing loss.[57] Another study has shown that, when taken together, magnesium and vitamins A, C, and E may help protect the ears from noise-induced hearing loss.[58] Scientists speculate that this combination of nutrients can still be effective even if they are only taken *after* the noise damage has been done. This means it's never too late to do what you can to slow or even reverse age-related hearing loss. Start by protecting your ears from loud noises whenever possible (for example, wear ear plugs when running a leaf blower). Increase your intake of folic acid, magnesium, and vitamins A, C, and E by taking supplements or eating more foods that are high in these nutrients.

Other common causes of hearing loss include arteriosclerosis, food allergies, thickening of ear passages, fluid congestion in the middle ear (reducing vibration), excess ear wax, mucous clog, infection or inflammation, swelling and congestion, chronic bronchial mastoid and sinus inflammation, hypoglycemia, a diet with too many mucous-forming foods, poor digestion (low HCL), poor circulation, high blood pressure, imbalance in the inner ear, low immune defenses, raised copper levels but low calcium levels, and, finally, metabolic imbalance.

Do you suffer from tinnitus (ringing in the ears)? So do 85 percent of hearing-loss sufferers. Ginkgo biloba extract, 60 mg taken three times daily for three months, may help alleviate the problem. You must be consistent for it to work. You should also keep your diet low in salt, dairy foods, caffeine, and sugar.

Support your hearing with:

▶ Folic acid
▶ Magnesium
▶ Vitamins A, C, and E
▶ Ginkgo biloba

life-extender tip

Wear earplugs to protect your ears from loud noises that can contribute to hearing loss as you age.

question

35

What substance do grapes contain that promotes longevity?

French cuisine is known for its rich sauces, gourmet cheeses, and fine wines. So, then, why do the French enjoy a relatively low incidence of coronary artery disease? The question may be finally answered in the fact that studies suggest that it may be the resveratrol, a constituent of red wine, that may have been protecting the French from the adverse health effects of their rich diet while also protecting their livers against the toxic effects of alcohol.[59] Could this be a French paradox solved? Just maybe.

answer

Resveratrol, a health-promoting compound found in grapes, has been shown to increase life span in several species. One of resveratrol's most studied applications involves the prevention of cardiovascular disease. This plant-derived compound appears to act through several different mechanisms to protect the cardiovascular system. Resveratrol may inhibit platelets from clumping together, thus reducing the risk of deadly blood clots that can lead to heart attack and stroke.

In addition to its cardioprotective effects, resveratrol exhibits a range of anticancer properties.

Resveratrol shows promise in protecting our brains and nervous systems against disorders associated with aging and genetic factors. In laboratory studies, resveratrol's antioxidant effect has been shown to protect against nerve cell damage caused by beta-amyloid peptide, which accumulates in the brains of Alzheimer's sufferers.

Here's more about this incredible substance: resveratrol may offer benefits in preventing or managing conditions associated with high blood sugar, such as metabolic syndrome or diabetes. Resveratrol is showing promise as a potential therapy for arthritis due to its ability to block the activity of inflammatory compounds.

While red wine does contain resveratrol, the quantity varies depending on where the grapes are grown, the time of harvest, and other factors. And drinking enough red wine to derive the optimal health benefits of resveratrol may not be practical or medically advisable.

It is suggested that one 100 mg resveratrol capsule per day can provide you with all of the protective benefits of this life-extending gift that has made front-page headlines around the world!

Resveratrol helps increase life span by:

▶ Cardio protection
▶ Anticancer properties
▶ Managing metabolic syndrome

life-extender tip

Take resveratrol today for a healthier tomorrow.

question

36

Could my thyroid make me feel more tired than usual?

Unrelenting fatigue, slow heart rate, cold hands and feet, moderate weight gain, swollen thyroid gland, hair loss, constipation, dry skin, poor memory, depression, and changes in personality are all signs that your thyroid gland may need a boost! If any of these symptoms sound familiar, a simple blood test can determine if you need to take action and support your "metabolic pacemaker."

answer

Thyroid problems are epidemic in proportion as we age. Thyroid disease affects nearly fifteen million people, with most sufferers being women. Among women over the age of sixty-five, one in ten has early stage hypothyroidism. Men are not immune to this metabolic monster, making up approximately one-fifth of persons that fall victim to this insidious condition that can make you feel older and actually age faster than necessary.[60] The reason doctors often miss so many cases of poor thyroid function is that the symptoms associated with thyroid disorder mimic the signs of aging. The range and severity of symptoms also vary greatly from one person to the next.

When your thyroid fails to produce enough thyroid hormone, your body's metabolism slows down, causing such symptoms as fatigue, lethargy, weight gain, mental sluggishness, and dry skin. This is called "hypothyroidism," which is the most common disorder concerning the thyroid. Thyroid conditions can be effectively treated with medication. It may take a few weeks or months to find just the right dose, or "sweet spot" as I like to call it, that will have you feeling like the you that you really are!

I should mention here that often the adrenal glands need support at the same time. Low adrenal function is often uncovered after a hypothyroid diagnosis and treatment is implemented. Vitamin C and B complex, licorice root, and ashwagandha can help to boost them, as well as Isocort, an adrenal glandular support formula. Isocort can be purchased from a nutritionally aware health-care provider or on the Internet when adrenal fatigue is suspected.

There are natural supplements that can help correct thyroid dysfunction. L-tyrosine plays a crucial role in supporting the thyroid gland. Tyrosine boosts your metabolism as well as acting as the precursor for dopamine, norepinephrine, and epinephrine, which are nervous system chemicals that affect metabolism, mental alertness, and energy levels. Tyrosine can be taken in supplement form with a meal that contains protein. If your doctor finds that you are suffering from hypothyroidism, you may take L-tyrosine with your thyroid medication. Make sure to keep your thyroid monitored with periodic blood tests; you may be able to reduce or eliminate the need for medication.

To make your thyroid happy:

▶ Have your TSH level checked.
▶ Have your blood tested for antibodies to check for Hashi-moto's thyroiditis (the primary cause of hypothyroidism).
▶ Do not take thyroid medication with iron supplements, because iron blocks the absorption of thyroid hormone.
▶ L-tyrosine may be taken along with thyroid medicine to boost low energy levels associated with hypothyroidism.

---

life-extender tip

Slowing down? Have your thyroid checked. Have your doctor screen you for Hashimoto's thyroiditis.

---

question

37

Can you tell me more about DHEA?

Scientists believe that the drop in levels of DHEA and the consequent drop of testosterone and estrogen may be related to many common age-related conditions, including diseases of the nervous, cardiovascular, and immune systems. Other conditions now believed to be related to diminished levels of DHEA and its end products include cancer, osteoporosis, and type 2 diabetes.

answer

DHEA (dehydroepiandrosterone) is a hormone that can be converted by the body to the hormones testosterone and estrogen.[61] Levels of DHEA are naturally very high among teens and young adults but begin to decrease by the early thirties. The typical seventy-year-old has DHEA levels only about 20 percent as high as he or she had in the early twenties.

So, restoring DHEA levels to those that naturally occur in younger adults may help slow the aging process and delay diseases of aging, such as heart disease, diabetes, and cancer. There is clinical evidence to back up this claim, including a study published in 2004 that showed reductions in abdominal fat and improvements in insulin sensitivity among older people who took DHEA for six months. I suggest you have a simple blood test to measure your DHEA levels. If they are low, the recommended dose for men is 50 mg per day and for women 15–20 mg per day.

While DHEA has demonstrated antiaging benefits, new evidence supports DHEA's critical role in relieving depression, enhancing endothelial function, preventing atherosclerosis, increasing bone mass, slowing osteoporosis, improving insulin resistance, and even hastening wound healing.

DHEA has both life-extending and life-enhancing benefits, but it is not for everyone. People with hormone-dependent cancers such as breast, uterine, and prostate cancers should avoid its use. With that being said, there is an abundance of evidence that suggests that ensuring that you have optimal levels of this vital "prohormone" can help aging adults guard against many debilitating conditions once thought to be the "inevitable" consequences of aging. Again, have your serum levels of DHEA tested by your health-care provider. If you are in fact low, you may want to consider boosting your levels to the optimal range by taking a DHEA supplement.

DHEA Serum Level Ranges		
	Normal Range	Optimal Range
Men	280–640	500–640
Women	65–380	250–380

DHEA can:

▶ Help slow the aging process
▶ Help increase bone mass
▶ Boost energy and well-being
▶ Delay the diseases of aging

life-extender tip
Make aging go away with DHEA!

Asparagus is a highly prized perennial vegetable that is considered a delicacy. A member of the lily family and originally from the eastern Mediterranean region, it is now grown commercially in countries such as the United States, Mexico, Peru, France, and Spain. It also provides beta-carotene, folic acid, phosphorus, potassium, and vitamins C, E, and K.

answer

The nutritional benefits of asparagus are tremendous—in particular its rich folate content, the B vitamin linked to a lower risk of heart disease. The slender spears boast healthy amounts of iron, vitamins A and C, and potassium. It also contains a special kind of carbohydrate called *insulin*. When our diet contains good amounts of insulin, the growth and activity of friendly bacteria increase, making it much more difficult for unfriendly bacteria to gain a foothold in our intestinal tract.

Here's more. Asparagus offers powerful protection against cancer because it contains a number of compounds that essentially double-team cancer-causing substances before they can do harm. In an analysis of thirty-eight vegetables, freshly cooked asparagus ranked first for its content of glutathione. This powerful substance helps to mop up free radicals that, when left unchecked, can run rampant through your body, causing damage to cells that can lead to cancer, atherosclerosis, and many other degenerative conditions.

Asparagus and Mushroom Pasta

1 lb. thin asparagus
3/4 lb. mushrooms (use your favorite)
2 Tbsp. extra-virgin olive oil
1/4 cup dry white wine
1/2 cup vegetable broth
4 Tbsp. unsalted butter
Sea salt and freshly ground black pepper
Fettuccine
1 Tbsp. flat leaf parsley

Cut off the tough ends of the asparagus and mushrooms and slice them into bite-size pieces.

In a large skillet, heat the oil over medium high heat; add mushrooms and cook, stirring until lightly browned. Add the asparagus and cook, stirring for two minutes. Add the wine and simmer until the liquid is evaporated. Add the vegetable broth and bring to a boil. Add the butter and toss until melted into the veggies. Season to taste.

In a large pot of boiling, salted water, cook pasta according to directions. Drain and transfer to a large bowl. Mix in the sauce and the parsley. Season to taste with additional salt and pepper.

Asparagus:

▶ Provides beta-carotene, folic aid, iron, phosphorus, potassium, and vitamins C, E, and K
▶ Lowers the risk of heart disease
▶ Offers powerful protection against cancer
▶ Contains glutathione, which helps mop up free radicals that can lead to many degenerative conditions

life-extender tip

Aging right means eating right! Start with a healthy serving of asparagus!

39

What is the proper amount of protein to consume daily?

Next to water, protein is your body's most plentiful substance and its primary source of building material for muscles, blood, skin, hair, nails, and organs like the heart and brain. The human body does not make protein, so it must be obtained through our diets. At times of high levels of stress, our protein needs can double in order to rebuild our worn-out system.

answer

Experts are now warning that Americans now eat too much protein for good health. Excessive protein consumption taxes your kidneys, is linked to urinary tract infections, and in diabetics can lead to serious kidney disease.

The premise of the current high-protein diet craze is that carbohydrates cause weight gain by releasing insulin, which stores fat. High-protein advocates say that, instead of eating carbohydrates, you should eat proteins, which will suppress your appetite and help you lose weight. But I say carbohydrates contribute to weight gain *only* when they don't contain fiber and when they are eaten in excess. In fact, fiber-rich carbohydrates such as whole-grain foods and fresh vegetables are the most filling foods with the fewest calories!

High-protein diets often restrict the intake of many grains, fruits, and some vegetables, which then limits our nutrient intake and can contribute to several diseases. For example, meat protein is high in saturated fat and cholesterol and is therefore strongly linked to cardiovascular disease and cancer.

Keep in mind that a high-protein diet (over 100 grams per day) can also weaken your bones because digesting and eliminating protein's by-products makes the body more acidic. This is especially true for red meat because of its tough, fibrous protein content that requires a lot of digestive acids to break it down. So again, it is wise to choose to get your daily protein requirement from vegetarian sources such as beans, peas, and soy foods. In addition to vegetarian sources, you may also get your quota from meats that are high in omega-3 fatty acids such as salmon and tuna for an added health benefit!

Here are daily protein requirements for optimal health:

Ages	Females	Males
11 to 14 years	46 grams	45 grams
15 to 18 years	44 grams	59 grams
19 to 24 years	46 grams	58 grams
Older than 25 years	50 grams	63 grams

Here's the scoop on protein!

▶ Get your protein from the plant kingdom when possible because it rarely contains saturated fat!

▶ Protein sources include lentils, beans, leafy greens, vegetables, and fruit.

▶ Other healthy protein sources include salmon and tuna.

life-extender tip

Make sure you don't get too much of a good thing! Use protein wisely to build you up, not tear you down!

question

40

Can you tell me what health benefits spinach provides?

We all know that Popeye made himself super strong by eating spinach, but you may be surprised to learn that he may also have been protecting himself against osteoporosis, heart disease, colon cancer, arthritis, and other diseases at the same time.

answer

Researchers have identified at least thirteen different flavonoid compounds in spinach that function as antioxidants and as anticancer agents. The anticancer properties of these spinach flavonoids have been shown to slow down cell division in stomach cancer cells and to reduce skin cancers. A study on adult women living in New England in the late 1980s also showed intake of spinach to be inversely related to incidence of breast cancer.

Here's more. Because spinach contains high levels of folate and vitamin B_{12}, it may protect the brain against dementia. Researchers from Tufts and Boston Universities observed subjects in the Framingham Heart Study and found those with high levels of homocysteine had nearly double the risk of developing Alzheimer's disease. High homocysteine is associated with low levels of folate and vitamins B_6, and B_{12}, leading researchers to speculate that getting more B vitamins may be protective.

Popeye's favorite stir-fry!

1 lb. beef eye of round
1 Tbsp. cornstarch

2 tsp. canola oil
2 tsp. grated fresh ginger
1 small onion, thinly sliced
1 bag (6 oz.) spinach, washed and trimmed
1/3 cup defatted beef broth
2 Tbsp. ketchup
Black pepper and sea salt, to taste

Cut the beef across the grain into very thin slices. Place in a medium bowl. Add cornstarch and toss to coat.

In a wok or large skillet, heat oil over medium high heat until it is nearly smoking. Add the beef and ginger. Stir-fry until the beef is no longer pink on the surface, about two minutes. Transfer to a plate.

Add the onion to the pan, and stir fry until softened, one to two minutes. Add the spinach and stir-fry until just wilted, about thirty seconds.

In a small bowl, combine the broth and ketchup. Add to the pan. Add the beef. Stir-fry until the sauce is heated through and coats the beef and vegetables, two to three minutes

Season to taste with sea salt and pepper. Serve over brown rice! Makes four servings, containing 207 calories each.

Eating spinach will supply you with:

▶ Antioxidants

▶ Folate

▶ Vitamins B_6 and B_{12}

▶ Flavonoids

life-extender tip

Eat spinach and be tough to the finish.

41 How can vinegar improve my health?

Hippocrates, the father of medicine, thought of vinegar as a powerful elixir and a naturally occurring antibiotic and antiseptic that fought germs. The ancient Egyptians and Greeks used it, and the Bible even mentions it as an antiseptic and healing agent. Even Columbus had barrels on his ships for the prevention of scurvy. Vinegar drinking is common practice in Japan, where it is widely accepted to help fight fatigue, improve circulation, and is generally good for overall health and vitality!

answer

What Grandma knew instinctively was that this inexpensive golden elixir is antibacterial, antifungal, and gives the immune system a boost. What we know these days is that vinegar is high in potassium and therefore is an electrolyte balancer. It "remineralizes" the body and helps normalize the body's alkaline-acid balance. In addition, it is good for aiding digestive upset, supporting urinary tract health, and helping to detoxify the liver. It provides enzymes, amino acids, and apple pectin (a source of dietary fiber).

The vinegar of choice when it comes to using vinegar therapeutically is apple cider vinegar, which is derived from fermented apple juice. It has no known side effects and is rich in vitamins C, E, A, P (bioflavonoids), B_1, B_2, and B_6; manganese; iron; calcium; sodium; magnesium; sulfur; copper; phosphorus; and silicon.

Vinegar has been studied for its ability to limit rising glucose levels following a meal. In 2005, Swedish researchers reported in the *European Journal of Clinical Nutrition* that the effect of vinegar on reducing the body's insulin response to a carbohydrate meal increases the feeling of satiety, a finding that could help dieters stick to their plan.[62] In addition, the acetic acid and butyric acid contained in vinegar support GI health by promoting the growth of friendly bifidobacteria. Vinegar also has both antiseptic and antibiotic properties and can be helpful in treating sore throat, cuts, wounds, digestive problems, and gum infections. There has been some suggestion that apple cider vinegar may help to reverse atherosclerosis (hardening of the arteries) and break up gallstones and kidney stones, possibly by dissolving calcium deposits. There is also some evidence to suggest that apple cider vinegar may have the potential to destroy both A and B strains of the human herpes virus-6 (HHV-6).

Add vinegar to your life by:

▶ Putting 2 Tbsp. in 8 oz. of water before a meal to help to curb your appetite

▶ Mixing 2 Tbsp. in 8 oz. of water and honey to help thin mucus associated with sinus infections and related sore throats. Sip this mixture throughout the day.

▶ Using it to help clear both internal and external yeast and fungal infections by either adding it to drinking water or, for women especially, applying it topically or douching with it

life-extender tip
Add vinegar, nature's solvent, to your diet today!

42

What are the health benefits of eating berries?

Scientists have found that berries have some of the highest antioxidant levels around, making them the most powerful (and delicious) disease-fighting foods available. The color pigments in berries are what give them these powerful antioxidants. Blue, purple, and red pigments have been associated with a lower risk of certain cancers, urinary tract infections, poor memory function, and the effects of aging. Consuming dietary fiber, which is found only in berries and other plant foods, also contributes to these health benefits.

answer

Berries, despite their tiny size, are powerful sources of phytochemicals—chemicals found in plants that have a variety of beneficial health effects. One phytochemical in particular is ellagic acid, which is believed to help prevent cellular changes that can lead to cancer. The good news is that *all* berries contain some ellagic acid, with strawberries and raspberries ranking among the top sources. Berries and the ellagic acid they contain may help fight cancer on several fronts, according to Gary Stoner, PhD, professor and cancer researcher at Ohio State University in Columbus, who has worked on a number of studies involving blackberries.[63]

A University of Georgia lab study found that phenolic compounds extracted from blueberries could limit colon cancer's ability to multiply and could also trigger renegade cells to die. Thus their findings suggest that blueberry intake may reduce colon cancer. Blueberries also appear to ward off deadly cancers, while protecting cells against damage caused by diabetes. Additional research suggests that consuming wild blueberries may help protect the brain against cell death due to ischemic stroke, which occurs when the brain is deprived of oxygen and can produce lasting damage to the nervous system.[64]

So you can see that berries are indeed a *berry* good thing! Add them to your favorite cereals, pancakes, salads, and baked goods such as pies!

Very Berry Sundae

    8 oz. raspberries
    12 oz. blueberries
    2 Tbsp. fresh orange juice
    1 Tbsp. honey
    1 tsp. vanilla extract
    ¼ tsp. almond extract
    1 pint fat-free vanilla frozen yogurt

Place half of the raspberries in a medium glass bowl. Mash lightly with a fork. Add the blueberries, orange juice, honey, vanilla, and almond extracts, as well as the remaining raspberries. Stir well to mix. Cover and let stand for at least thirty minutes to allow the flavors to blend.

Scoop the frozen yogurt into four dessert dishes. Stir the berry mixture and spoon over the yogurt.

Makes four wonderful servings at only 170 calories each.

Berries are:

▶ Powerful sources of phytochemicals
▶ Helpful cancer fighters
▶ Brain and cell protectors

life-extender tip

Make berries a part of your antiaging arsenal!

43

Do apples have cardioprotective benefits?

When John Chapman, aka "Johnny Appleseed," wandered around the eastern states and the Midwest during the 1800s planting apple seeds and establishing apple orchards, he did not realize that his efforts inadvertently helped to improve Americans' health. Since Johnny's days, research has shown that eating apples can reduce the risk of heart disease, protect you from lung cancer, lower your risk of asthma, and protect overall lung function.

answer

Apples are high in antioxidants, which have been linked to better heart health. In addition to being a delicious and flexible ingredient, apples have also been linked to a reduced risk of heart damage in laboratory studies. Eating apples and apple products has been linked to providing protection from cellular damage that otherwise could have led to an increased risk of heart disease and certain cancers. One apple, or even more, just may keep the doctor away. Consider these apple nutrition facts:

▶ Apples are a natural source of health-promoting phytonutrients, a plant-based antioxidant that promotes bone health.

▶ Apples contain natural fruit sugars, mostly in the form of fructose, and because of an apple's high-fiber content, the fruit's natural sugars are slowly released into the bloodstream, helping maintain steady blood sugar levels.

▶ Apples are an excellent source of fiber, containing both soluble and insoluble fiber.

▶ Apples are fat free, saturated fat free, sodium free, and cholesterol free.

There are many other health benefits that scientists believe are linked to eating apples and apple products, from Alzheimer's disease to breast cancer and weight loss.

Speaking of weight loss, the insoluble fiber, found mostly in the skin, is the kind we call roughage, which has long been recommended to prevent constipation. In addition, insoluble fiber is very filling, which is why the apple is a wonderful weight-control food for those of you who want to lose weight without feeling hungry.

Concerning lung health, a study in the Netherlands found that those who ate more apples and pears had better lung function and less chronic obstructive pulmonary disease. Apples are high in quercetin, an exceptional antioxidant that helps prevent harmful oxygen molecules from damaging individual cells. Consequently, apples may also help ward off lung cancer. Finnish researchers found that men who consumed more quercetin were 60 percent less likely to have lung cancer than men with lower quercetin intakes.[65]

Apples can help:

▶ Lower the risk of heart disease
▶ Prevent constipation
▶ Improve lung function
▶ Lower the risk of lung cancer

life-extender tip

Red, green, sweet, or tart, have an apple today to protect your heart!

Why does brown rice offer more benefits than white rice?

There are an estimated forty thousand varieties of rice worldwide. It is the most widely used ingredient in most cooks' pantries! The most nutritious kind of rice is brown rice, which contains an abundant amount of fiber, complex carbohydrates, and essential B vitamins.

answer

Often called "nature's digestive sponge," brown rice is darker and chewier than its lighter colored cousin because it's wrapped in a nutritious outer skin that is higher in fiber. A half-cup of brown rice contains about 2 grams of fiber. This means that brown rice offers protection against type 2 diabetes, reduces cholesterol, keeps digestion regular, and lowers the risk of colon and breast cancer. This is because the fiber in brown rice is the insoluble kind that acts like a sponge in your intestines, soaking up water, which causes stools to get larger and wetter so they pass more quickly and more easily. This simply means that any harmful substances that your colon contains has less time to damage cells in your colon wall, which in turn may reduce your risk of colon cancer.

Eating a serving of whole grains, such as brown rice, at least six times each week is an especially good idea for postmenopausal women with high cholesterol, high blood pressure, or other signs of cardiovascular disease (CVD). A three-year prospective study of over two hundred postmenopausal women with CVD, published in the *American Heart Journal*, shows that those eating at least six servings of whole grains each week experienced both slowed progression of atherosclerosis, the buildup of plaque that narrows the vessels through which blood flows, and less progression in stenosis, the narrowing of the diameter of arterial passageways. The women's intake of fiber from fruits, vegetables, and refined grains was *not* associated with a lessening in CVD progression.[66] A compound in the bran layer of the rice called oryzanol has been shown to reduce the body's production of cholesterol. Oryzanol is chemically similar to cholesterol-lowering medications. Eating at least three servings a day of whole grains, especially brown rice, can cut your risk for heart disease, cancer, obesity, and diabetes.

Brown rice offers:

▶ Diabetes protection

▶ Abundant fiber

▶ Help in lowering cholesterol

▶ Help with digestion

▶ Cardiovascular protection

life-extender tip

Use nature's "sponge" to reduce cholesterol, keep digestion regular, and lower the risk of colon and breast cancer!

45 Is it true that yams are hormone precursors?

Sweet potatoes and yams are a rich source of DHEA. This important precursor hormone can become estrogen, testosterone, or progesterone as needed in the body. The problem is, as we age, our body's level of DHEA drops, which hampers our body's anti-aging defenses. By adding sweet potatoes and yams to your diet on a regular basis, you will receive high amounts of beta-carotene, vitamin C, protein, and fiber, as well as DHEA, which all work in symphony to keep you young, vibrant, and full of energy.

answer

One of the best friends that a woman can have during the perimenopausal/menopausal years is the sweet potato. Not only is this bright, luscious, velvety little powerhouse packed with DHEA, but it is also packed with vitamin A to boost resistance to infections and allergies, lots of the B and C vitamins to help women handle anxiety and stress and fight fatigue, plus carotenoids to protect her body from free radical damage.

Many studies have shown that a woman's risk for stroke may be cut when she eats a sweet potato every day. This is more reason to reach for this orange tuber to keep you feeling super!

Sweet potatoes are a good source of fiber, so they are a very healthy food for people with diabetes. The fiber indirectly helps lower blood sugar levels by slowing down the rate at which food is absorbed into the bloodstream. And because sweet potatoes are high in complex carbohydrates, they can help people control their weight, which also helps keep diabetes under control.

Because sweet potatoes contain the B vitamins folate and B_6, they may give the brain a boost in performing its functions, which sometimes diminish with age.

When buying sweet potatoes, always choose those with the most intense, lush orange color because the richer the color, the greater the jolt of beta-carotene. Store your "sweeties" at room temperature to lengthen their shelf life. Make sure not to get them wet, as they will spoil. Wash them when you are ready to cook them. Once baked, sweet potatoes will keep in your refrigerator for seven to ten days. To prepare them for baking, simply scrub them, dry them, and pierce the skins in several places with a fork. Place them on a baking sheet because they will drip juices during the baking process. Bake at 350 degrees for one hour. For an added treat, sprinkle with cinnamon and brown sugar and a little butter! I often have this for dessert!

Sweet potatoes can help:

▶ Preserve memory
▶ Control diabetes
▶ Reduce the risk of heart disease and cancer
▶ Provide a good source of fiber

life-extender tip

Not just for holidays anymore! Have a sweet potato today—only 117 calories per 4-ounce serving!

Hippocrates once said, "Let thy food be thy medicine and thy medicine be thy food." Eating a whole-food live diet is like a preventative medicine in that it promotes health by decreasing fats and sugar intake while increasing fiber and nutrient intake. In addition, it means more satisfaction and less overeating. Also, whole-food diets are low in fat and cholesterol but high in essential nutrients—unlike foods many Americans normally eat that rob the body rather than nourish it; for example, refined sugars, commercial colas, refined-grain flours and pastas, processed fats, hydrogenated fats such as margarine, and deep-fried foods. Refined sugars, when consumed in excess, decrease immunity, increase risk of heart disease and obesity, promote dental decay, aggravate hyperactive behavior in some children, and provide no nutritional value at all. So where do you start?

answer

A whole-food diet is generously filled with live foods in their whole state. This is the way we were intended to eat to experience optimal and vibrant health—different colored vegetables and fruits; grains; raw seeds, nuts, and their butters; beans; fermented dairy products like yogurt and kefir; fish; poultry; and bean products like tofu. Your diet should be lower in cheeses and fats as well as animal meats. By eating a whole-food diet, you will be consuming a diet that is high in foods as whole as possible with the least amount of processed, adulterated, fried, or sweetened additives.

Did you know that many of the foods at your local grocery store have been picked or slaughtered weeks or even *months* before they reach your store? They are often artificially preserved or treated with nitrogen to help deter spoilage. The longer it takes for foods to get to your table means less nutrients for you and your family.

The answer? Start shopping at farmer's markets whenever possible. At these markets, many times, you can actually meet the farmer. Imagine that!

Life replenishes life—your life!

▶ Eat more high-protein plant foods—nuts, grains, seeds, and legumes.

▶ Choose free-range, hormone-free, additive-free meats.

▶ Have rhythm to your diet. Eating regularly provides your body with a consistent intake of nutrient-dense foods and will therefore prevent you from overeating and reaching for "dead," overprocessed, sugar-laden foods.

▶ Eat fresh and in season.

life-extender tip

Add fresh, whole, organic foods to your diet. Life replenishes life! Make it a point to stop eating "dead foods" that are laden with preservatives, dyes, hormones, and pesticides.

47

Can you tell me the benefits of systematic undereating?

People who eat less or practice the three-fourths rule, eating only until your stomach is three-fourths full, may live more years. It is true that we need to eat more of certain nutrient-dense foods as we age, but "caloric restriction" (CR) can help extend your life and help slow down the aging process. Many experts believe that caloric restriction "resets" your metabolism so it works more efficiently, and your body shifts its focus from growth and reproduction to long-term survival. When you take in fewer calories, your body naturally produces fewer free radicals as it turns food into energy. This will result in less oxidative damage. This does not mean to starve yourself. It simply means to choose whole foods that are nutrient dense. Eliminate junk foods from your life, and stop eating before you are full and overstuffed!

answer

Eating smaller meals four or five times a day will deliver to your system a steady supply of nutrients that will help keep your blood sugar balanced and will give you boundless energy throughout the day. As I mentioned, eating less and now making sure that you are eating smaller meals will be less taxing on your metabolic and digestive systems as well as prevent you from overloading your system with excess wastes. Excess wastes in the body can be a breeding ground for disease.

In a study conducted on a variety of laboratory animals, CR has been shown to dramatically extend life span.[67] While it may break the "social ties that bind us to food," the promise of living healthier and longer may help you do just that!

CR is also referred to as "undernutrition without malnutrition." CR refers to a normal, healthy diet with one modification: the reduction in your diet's caloric content, anywhere from 10 percent for a noticeable effect to as much as 40 percent to 50 percent for a maximum effect. When I say maximum effect, I mean for the purpose of slowing aging and, therefore, extending life.

There are many advocates of CR. First, those on calorie-restricted healthy diets enjoy an immediate reduction in the risk of dying from age-related illnesses such as cancer, heart disease, and adult-onset diabetes.[68] This may not matter to you if you have been blessed with great genes, but for others not so fortunate, CR could be a lifesaver!

If you consider CR, it is important for you to weigh the cost now of forgoing large meals and not indulging in unhealthy food choices with the potential of minimizing your risk of disease in the future. The choice is yours!

Practicing caloric restriction can:

▶ Reduce your risk of dying from age-related illnesses
▶ Manage your weight
▶ Reset your metabolism

life-extender tip
Eat less to live long!

48

Is the hype about the benefits of pomegranate juice true?

The amazing pomegranate represents longevity and immortality in many ancient cultures. But today's research shows that it can really help prevent the most common health problems associated with aging, particularly heart disease. This truly amazing fruit addresses several aspects of heart disease, including atherosclerosis, blood flow, LDL oxidation, and high blood pressure. Laboratory research suggests that it may also be effective in cancer prevention, diabetes, neurological health, infection, and osteoarthritis.

answer

Pomegranates have long been used in folk medicine around the world to treat cuts, sore throats, diarrhea, gum disease, and infections. Hippocrates used them for treating fevers.

Today, the pomegranate is widely recognized for its antioxidant properties. Studies show that the pomegranate has more antioxidant power than any of the foods typically recommended as antioxidants, including blueberries, cranberries, red wine, and green tea. It is also more powerful acting than the common antioxidants vitamins A, C, and E. Pomegranates' antioxidant properties are attributed to its high content of soluble polyphenols, including a tannin called punicalagin. Punicalagins are the major component responsible for the antioxidant and health benefits of pomegranate juice.[69]

Most of the studies on the pomegranate have focused on its effect on heart disease. Clinical studies in humans have focused on the pomegranate's ability to prevent and treat atherosclerosis, diabetes, osteoarthritis, and cancer. A few studies have also documented the pomegranate's antibacterial and antiviral effects.

Can pomegranates reverse heart disease? They really can, according to recent studies.

The majority of recent studies on the health benefits of pomegranates have explored their ability to stop and even reverse the buildup of plaque in arteries. These studies show that pomegranates offer significant health benefits for people at risk for heart disease. It has been suggested that pomegranates combat atherosclerosis by stimulating paraoxonase (PON) enzyme activity and HDL-associated protein. Animal studies show that polyphenols inhibit LDL oxidation and reduce atherosclerosis, thus reducing the risk for cardiovascular problems such as heart attack and stroke.

In addition to its cardiovascular protection, pomegranates offer help for osteoarthritis by inhibiting cartilage breakdown.[70] Researchers have identified two antidementia components in pomegranates: ellagic acid and punicalagin. Both of these components seem to inhibit a serine protease associated with dementia.[71]

When you add in all of the other benefits, which include improved immune functioning, neurological health, and protection against cancer and osteoarthritis, you can see how truly amazing the pomegranate really is!

The amazing pomegranate can:

▶ Help prevent and reverse heart disease
▶ Help prevent dementia
▶ Inhibit cartilage breakdown associated with osteoarthritis

life-extender tip

Have an 8 oz. glass of pomegranate juice each day or take one 200 mg capsule daily.

49

Does sesame oil have anticancer properties?

It's time to open your mind to sesame! Get ready to experience this refined, nutty, aromatic flavor either as an oil that you cook with or by simply sprinkling sesame seeds on your favorite salads or casseroles. The health benefits are plentiful. Just ask the many Chinese people who are enjoying long, healthy lives. Most of them have used sesame all of their lives. Chinese medicine holds that sesame is a blood builder, a kidney and liver tonic, as well as a bowel protector and regulator. Sesame is a great source of phytic acid, an antioxidant that may help to prevent cancer.

answer

Here are more reasons to add sesame to your life: Sesame seeds aid in digestion, stimulate blood circulation, and benefit the nervous system. They are a great source of iron and zinc. Include sesame seeds in your diet if you are a vegan, because many vegans do not get enough iron or zinc from their meals. Sesame seeds protect your body from free radicals, and its phytic acid content helps inhibit colon cancer. The compound sesamin protects your liver from oxidative damage and also helps to relieve constipation. One-half cup of sesame seeds contains three times more calcium than one-half cup of milk!

To help get you started, here's one of my favorite sesame health-building recipes.

Dr. Janet's Sweet Sesame Potatoes

2 pounds sweet potatoes
2 tsp. sesame seeds

1 bunch scallions, chopped
2 cloves garlic, minced
1 Tbsp. olive oil
1 Tbsp. Bragg Liquid Aminos
1 Tbsp. packed light brown sugar
1 tsp. dark sesame oil

Scrub the sweet potatoes and pat dry with paper towels. With a fork, pierce each potato in three or four places. Place the potatoes, in spoke fashion and with the thinner ends pointing toward the center, on a paper towel in a microwave oven. Microwave on high power for five minutes. Turn the potatoes. Microwave for five to nine minutes more, or until the potatoes can be easily pierced with the tip of a sharp knife but are still firm. Set aside until cool enough to handle. Peel, then cut into thick slices.

Place the sesame seeds in a large nonstick skillet. Stir over medium heat for thirty seconds or until golden. Stir in the scallions, olive oil, and garlic. Cook for thirty seconds longer or until fragrant. Add the Bragg Liquid Aminos, brown sugar, and dark sesame oil. Cook until the sugar melts, about ten seconds. Add the sweet potatoes to the pan, and toss to coat. Cook for one minute to heat through. Makes six servings.

Add sesame to your diet to:

► Aid digestion
► Benefit your nervous system
► Relieve constipation
► Protect your liver from oxidative damage
► Add flavor to your life

life-extender tip

Add sesame seeds to your food today. You may also stir-fry in sesame oil!

Why I should take a probiotic every day?

Probiotics are beneficial bacteria in your intestinal tract that can improve your health by maintaining and boosting your gastrointestinal and immune system function. Probiotics act with a part of your small intestine called the Peyer's patches, which directly tell your immune system to be vigilant. Probiotics produce volatile fatty acids that provide metabolic energy. In addition, they help you digest food and amino acids, produce certain vitamins, and, most importantly, make your lower intestine mildly acidic, thus inhibiting the growth of bad bacteria such as *E. coli*, which has caused serious illnesses in recent years.

answer

Probiotic supplementation is absolutely essential in your fight against candida or any fungal infection because of the antifungal properties that these "natural defenders" possess.

All of us have needed an antibiotic at one time or another during the course of our lives. Yeast infections, gastrointestinal distress, and diarrhea have plagued millions of us who have had to resort to taking them. While antibiotics may have helped to wipe out an infection by killing off the bad bacteria, unfortunately, our good bacteria was assaulted as well, leaving us without the full arsenal of gastrointestinal protection that probiotics supply.

According to the best-selling book *Prescription for Nutritional Healing*, the flora in a healthy colon should consist of at least 85 percent *lactobacilli* and 15 percent coliform bacteria.[72] The typical colon bacteria count today is the reverse, which has resulted in gas, bloating, intestinal and systemic toxicity, constipation, and malabsorption of nutrients, making our colons perfect breeding grounds for the overgrowth of candida.

If you are currently on antibiotic therapy, it is vitally important that you supplement your digestive tract with probiotics because antibiotic use destroys your healthy bowel flora along with the bacteria that is being killed off. This will normalize and restock your intestinal pond with the healthy flora that will keep your immunity up and your yeast count and resultant gastrointestinal distress down!

I recommend that you make it a point to add probiotics to your daily life-extension ritual. While you may take them in a powder, capsule, or liquid form, I believe that in addition to these sources, you should try to obtain them from food sources whenever possible. These sources include yogurt, buttermilk, goat's milk, miso, kimchi, and sauerkraut. For optimum probiotic activity, look for yogurts that contain *bifidobacterium* and/or *lactobacilli*.

If you are on the go, there are some probiotic drink mixes that can be found at your local health food store that contain beneficial probiotic organisms.

Probiotics can:

▶ Help manage food allergies
▶ Strengthen your immunity
▶ Fortify your intestinal tract

life-extender tip

Today, add probiotics to your daily life-extending regimen. Yogurt, buttermilk, soy milk, and sauerkraut are wonderful sources. You may also take probiotics in a capsule, powdered, or liquid form. Look for lactobacillus and acidophilus at your local health food or grocery store in the refrigerator section.

51

Can folate safeguard me from cardiovascular disease?

Folate-rich, dark green leafy vegetables, beans, and asparagus may play a major role in preventing heart attacks and so much more! Food sources that contain folate include asparagus, artichokes, avocados, beets, broccoli, lentils, orange juice, spinach, and sweet potatoes. Folate is a B vitamin that has many longevity-promoting benefits. Making sure that you are getting enough folate in your diet can help protect you from cardiovascular disease. High homocysteine levels are an important contributor to heart disease, and it appears that it can be brought down to safe levels easily with modest amounts of folate added to your diet.

answer

Studies have shown that people with the most folate in their blood are the ones least likely to develop colon cancer, particularly cigarette smokers, as reported by the Karolinska Institute in Sweden and the Harvard School of Public Health.[73] To clarify the possible influence of smoking on folate's protective effect against colon cancer, the study followed more than sixty-one thousand women. Using food frequency questionnaires, the researchers determined mean daily folate intake among the study subjects to be 183 mcg.

During nearly fifteen years of follow-up, 805 cases of colorectal cancer were documented in the study group. Women who ingested less than 150 mcg of folate daily had a 39 percent greater risk of colon cancer compared to women who consumed at least 212 mcg of folate daily. A dose-related response relationship was observed between daily folate intake and colon cancer risk, predicting that each 100-mcg increase in folate intake could decrease colon cancer risk by 34 percent. Among women who had smoked cigarettes for ten or more years, those consuming at least 193 mcg of folate daily had a 66 percent lower risk of colon cancer than those whose folate intake was less than 163 mcg. Although nonsmokers with the lowest folate intake had a 41 percent lower risk of colon cancer than did smokers, smokers with the highest folate intake had the same risk of colon cancer as nonsmokers with the highest folate intake.

What does this mean to you? Simply this. Increasing dietary folate intake may decrease the risk of colon cancer. This is especially notable in smokers, who experience an elevated risk for the disease.

In addition, studies are now pointing to possible connections between folate intake and the risk of cognitive problems, particularly Alzheimer's disease.[74]

Folate:

▶ Reduces risk of cancers
▶ Lowers homocysteine levels
▶ May boost cognitive function

life-extender tip

Add 400–600 mcg of folate to your life-extending protocol today! Make sure to add folate to your plate!

52

Can I be headed for "burnout" even if I feel fine right now?

How have you spent most of your life up until now? Have you been chasing wealth and neglecting your health? Today it is time to realize that if you continue living this way, you will switch from wealth chasing to health chasing as you age. Slow down, and take charge of YOU. That is why I have written these one hundred answers on how to live longer—and better. Begin today to breathe deeply, laugh with friends, take a day of rest, and be grateful for who you are and how far you have come. Eat fresh, sleep enough, drink plenty of water, whatever you love—do it!

answer

There are very clear guidelines when it comes to preventing degenerative disease and extending your life. They are as follows:

▶ Go to bed by 10:00 p.m. whenever possible and sleep in until 9:00 a.m. These are the hours in which your body repairs, rebuilds, and recovers. It is between the hours of 10:00 p.m. and 9:00 a.m. that your adrenal glands get much needed rest and recovery time. While sleeping in until 9:00 a.m. is not practical for those of us who work or have small children, you should try to do it on weekends.

▶ Manage any chronic pain. Chronic pain interferes with life and vitality. If you have back pain, neck pain, headaches, and/or muscle stiffness, you should know that your body is sending you very clear signals that you need to take action to manage or eliminate any stressors, both mental or physical that may have contributed to your pain syndrome. See a massage therapist or chiropractor, exercise, or see an orthopedic health-care provider. Don't just "live with it." Take action. Pain robs you of energy and saps your spirit.

▶ Limit simple sugars, and avoid foods that spike your blood sugar. Eat low-glycemic foods that will help keep your blood sugar levels steady throughout the day. Have protein and a complex carbohydrate at each meal.

▶ Limit caffeine and alcohol. Both, when used in excess, can rob your body of precious nutrients.

▶ Say no to things that you do not want to do. It is OK! Purge your life of "energy robbers," whether it be a person, place, or thing—in other words, anything that takes life away from you.

▶ Make daily deposits into your "happiness bank account." Take time to do something each day that gives you joy. Many people who experience illness live imbalanced lives. What's your hurry? Life is not a race. It is a journey that is meant to be savored!

To extend life:

▶ Sleep enough and eat healthy.
▶ Slow down and savor life's flavor.
▶ Make time for YOU!

life-extender tip
Slow down. Don't go so fast. You want to make this lifetime last!

question

53

What is the danger concerning plastic?

It is time for us to get back to basics. Plastic is probably one of the greatest inventions this world has ever known. It is virtually in every aspect of our lives—TVs, computers, water bottles, packaging, cosmetics, chewing gum, carpeting, upholstery, toilet paper, and so much more. While plastic has been a durable, convenient, and versatile "family member" to us all, it is now known that this old friend is not as "friendly" as we once thought. Plastics are known sources of xenoestrogens, or estrogen "mimics" that can wreak havoc on the hormonal balances of men, women, and children, causing estrogen dominance. In addition, plastics release vinyl chloride and other potentially dangerous gases that can be linked to birth defects, cancer, liver, and lung disease.

answer

There is much concern over the chemical bisphenol A (or BPA) that has some scientists and health experts worried. BPA is found in plastic containers such as water bottles and baby bottles. According to the National Toxicology Program (NTP), part of the National Institutes of Health, a study found reason for "some concern" that bisphenol A could possibly have neural and behavioral effects on fetuses, infants, and children.[75]

Based mainly on rat studies, the effects of this chemical that mimics estrogen are believed to act on mammary glands and reproductive organs, causing earlier puberty. The researchers were most concerned about exposed fetuses and children because they are still undergoing rapid development of a variety of body systems.

The risk to adults at this point was negligible, the NTP said, because most human exposure to BPA comes from some polycarbonate plastics with a number 7 on the bottom, some drink containers, and the lining of some cans.

Interesting, though, is that while the FDA has long said that the "leaching" of BPA in tiny amounts is "safe," they are now reviewing this study and report.[76]

Others have chosen not to wait but to act now. Officials in Canada announced a federal ban on baby bottles that contain BPA. Wal-Mart plans to remove the plastics from U.S. stores by early 2009.

The company that makes Nalgene water bottles said they are going to stop making their polycarbonate water bottles that contain BPA.

Minimize health risks by replacing all of your plastics with:

▶ Glass
▶ Wood
▶ Cotton
▶ Paper products from recycled paper

life-extender tip

Plastics are a controversy until more research is unveiled. The choice is yours—paper or plastic?

54

What can I do to get rid of yeast infections once and for all?

Are you tired, achy, bloated, suffering from yeast infections, or have been on repeated courses of antibiotics? Do you crave sugar, carbs, pies, cakes, and pastries? If so, you may be suffering from yeast overgrowth, a commonly underdiagnosed, underrecognized condition. Yeast overgrowth is not a simple yeast infection. It is often a tenacious, unwelcome guest that takes a major intervention to rid your system of. Yeast overgrowth contributes to malabsorption of food and malnutrition if you do not take the steps necessary to eradicate it from your system.

answer

It is *candida albicans* that causes what is known as the common yeast-related syndrome called *candidiasis*. It is a stress-related condition marked by a compromised immune response. Once yeast colonies establish a foothold and flourish, they release toxins into your bloodstream that trigger many symptoms such as constipation, diarrhea, colitis, bloating, muscle and joint pain, clogged sinuses, vaginitis, kidney and bladder problems, memory loss and mood swings, low blood sugar, low thyroid, hormone imbalances, prostatitis, foggy thinking, fatigue, weight gain or loss, and many more.

Dietary consideration for taming the "yeast beast"

The candida eradication diet permits dense protein foods such as chicken and fish and as many vegetables as you can eat. While some people can tolerate whole grains, most cannot. Caffeine and alcohol should be avoided, as should foods made from white flour: breads, pasta, flour tortillas, cakes, cookies, and so on. Eliminate all sugar and sugar-containing foods. Read food labels carefully, because thousands of packaged foods contain sucrose, dextrose, glucose, fructose, corn syrup, maple syrup, honey, molasses, barley malt, rice syrup, and more. If sweetening is required, simply use stevia.

Drink only filtered or glass-bottled water because tap water contains chlorine, which will further reduce your body's population of good bacteria.

While the candida diet is rigid, it is necessary. Once you tame this beast, you will be able to slowly add in grains and low-sugar fruits such as Granny Smith apples.

Be careful to monitor the way you feel, so you will be able to nip yeast in the "bud" before it nips you!

Plan your attack against yeast by:

▶ Avoiding antibiotics unless absolutely necessary, using instead natural antibiotics such as olive leaf extract, oil of oregano, grapefruit seed extract, and garlic extract

▶ Detoxifying your body to cleanse dead yeast from your system

▶ Using enzyme therapy to strengthen your digestive system; "restock" your intestinal pond with friendly bacteria such as *Lactobacillus acidophilus* and *Lactobacillus bifidus*

▶ Rebuilding immunity

▶ Making diet changes as outlined above

▼ life-extender tip

Add yeast-fighting nutrients to your daily diet such as unsweetened yogurt, garlic, caprylic acid, grapefruit seed extract, oil of oregano, and olive leaf extract. These all may be found at your local health food store.

55 What makes alpha lipoic acid such a powerful antioxidant?

When it comes to antioxidant protection, alpha lipoic acid is the "king" of your body's universe. In other words, this universal antioxidant has an ability unlike any other antioxidant, which is to work in both fatty and water internal body environments. When your body uses up vitamin E and C during stressful life events, alpha lipoic acid has the ability to convert the by-products into new antioxidant compounds by "recycling" the vitamins. Alpha lipoic acid provides great benefit and protection from nerve damage in diabetics and persons with Alzheimer's and Parkinson's disease. It offers protection from most age-related diseases, including cancer, cardiovascular disease, and cataracts.

answer

Here's more—alpha lipoic acid boosts the levels of glutathione (an essential antioxidant), which is universally recognized as crucial to overall health and immunity. Optimal levels of these universal antioxidants are necessary to maintain youthful structure and function of the body's mitochondria (energy powerhouses found in every cell), which may be associated with increased longevity!

Although alpha lipoic acid is not considered a weight-loss agent, it does seem to have effects that may be worth investigating. Some researchers have done it for you. Studies have shown that this universal antioxidant can decrease fat accumulation in mice. Alpha lipoic acid also reduces body weight and prevents the development of diabetes in diabetes-prone obese rats by reducing triglyceride accumulation in nona-dipose tissues, thereby improving insulin sensitivity.[77] From a general health and longevity standpoint, it is wise to add alpha lipoic acid to your arsenal. If your waistline shrinks in the process, even better!

As the amount of alpha lipoic acid produced by your body decreases with age, supplementation is necessary to maintain adequate levels. Scientific studies showing the benefits of alpha lipoic acid have used doses ranging from 300–500 mg daily. To reap the most benefit, take your alpha lipoic acid with biotin and a vitamin B complex.

Alpha lipoic acid has a wide range of benefits, including preventing and treating atherosclerotic vascular diseases, helping to slow the progression of neurodegenerative diseases such as Alzheimer's disease, and having possible anticancer effects. Some of the most impressive research on alpha lipoic acid involves its role in fighting type 2 diabetes. Numerous studies have shown that alpha lipoic acid improves glucose tolerance as well as the peripheral nerve complications associated with full-blown diabetes.

Alpha lipoic acid:

- ▶ Deters the development of diabetes, Alzheimer's, and Parkinson's disease
- ▶ Offers protection from cancer, cardiovascular disease, and cataracts
- ▶ Boosts glutathione levels
- ▶ Decreases fat accumulation and reduces body weight
- ▶ Aids in the prevention and treatment of atherosclerotic vascular diseases

life-extender tip

Power up! Add alpha lipoic acid to your antiaging arsenal.

Juices are some of *the* most powerful whole foods you can put into your body. They take very little effort to digest, so you can benefit almost instantly from all of the energy and nutrients they provide. Your body absorbs nutrients from juices better than it does from the foods themselves because you break down the plant's cellulose, which makes all of the health-promoting vitamins, minerals, and other healing compounds easier to absorb. Juices give you more nutritional bang for the buck!

answer

▼

Unless you chew your food very well, and few people do, you will not get all the nutrients from food that you can get from juice.

Juices also provide a wonderful array of phytonutrients, which are compounds in plants that may help ward off serious age-related diseases such as heart disease, cancer, and Alzheimer's.

Juicing offers you the added benefit of helping to control your weight. Drinking fresh juices leaves you feeling satisfied and therefore will help you limit excessive food intake.

To get the most from your juicing efforts, use fresh, ripe, organic produce; sip your juice quickly and drink it within thirty minutes of making it for optimal enzyme activity. Drink it thirty minutes *before* a large meal so that all the nutrients are absorbed. Juice a variety of vegetables for maximum healing benefits. Be creative!

While fruit juices are wonder cleansers for your body's systems, and they are OK once in a while, they contain a lot of sugar. That is why I suggest you do not make them your first juice of choice. You should focus on vegetables. They are low in sugar and better nutritionally because they have a higher alkaline content than fruit juices, which tend to be acidic. You may, however, add an apple to your vegetable juice to sweeten it.

Here are some of my favorite juice recipes that have therapeutic properties: For constipation, combine carrot and spinach juice. For arthritis, you can try grapefruit juice, carrot and spinach juice, or celery juice. Cabbage juice, as well as a combination of carrot, beet, and cucumber juice, is great for ulcers. For nervous tension, try mixing carrot and celery juice. You'll wake up and be energized with carrot, beet, and cucumber juice. A parsley, spinach, celery, and carrot juice combo will ease your headaches.

Tip: Combining the juice from a couple of tomatoes with the juice from a few slices of green bell peppers makes a great refreshing low-sodium alternative to commercial tomato juice drinks.

Juicing can:

▶ Help prevent cancer and heart disease

▶ Boost immunity

▶ Lower your risk of Alzheimer's disease

▶ Cleanse your body of toxins

life-extender tip

Pour yourself a "glass of health." Add fresh juices to your diet.

57 How can my problem with bloating and indigestion be solved?

If you are like most people, you do not chew your food very well. Digestion begins in the mouth, starting with an enzyme called ptyalin. Its job is to help "predigest" your food so that your stomach does not have to work so hard. When you take the time to chew your food well, you not only relieve the stomach of a much harder task of breaking down your meal, but you are also getting the chance to savor all of the flavor in each bite of food you take. Life is meant to be enjoyed. Eating is one of our pleasures, not to be rushed or hurried. It is no wonder Americans are popping antacids, the "pink stuff," the "purple pill," and more! Slow down and chew. Let your body take in all of your food's vitamins, minerals, and nutrients in the way that God designed. Remember, savor the flavor!

answer

If you have digestive upsets or difficulty digesting food, chew sixty times per mouthful. The instructions are very simple: chew, chew, chew! For those who have normal digestion, you still must chew at least thirty times, if possible, before swallowing.

If you are counting calories, listen up! A University of Rhode Island study has shown that eating slow and chewing each bite fifteen to twenty times can help you lose weight, leaves you physically satisfied longer, and makes a meal more enjoyable. Thirty college-age women had plates of pasta and were told to begin eating. First, they were told to eat quickly. When evaluated, it was found that they consumed

646 calories over the course of nine minutes. But when they were told to slow down and chew each bite fifteen to twenty times, their caloric intake dropped dramatically to 579 calories in twenty-nine minutes.[78] Not bad, wouldn't you say, for a simple mechanical change.

If you are diabetic, chew one hundred times per mouthful, because the more thorough the chewing, the more completely the food particles are mixed with your saliva, which contains enzymes needed for digestion. In addition, the act of chewing is a relaxing one—making mealtime a pleasant and more fun restorative process that will benefit your entire body. Eating and the act of eating then become therapeutic in themselves. So it is actually good to "chew your cabbage twice"!

Chewing your food well:

▶ Aids digestion

▶ Contributes to less calorie consumption

▶ Helps your body deliver more nutrients to your system

life-extender tip

Today and every day, focus on chewing each bite of food twenty to thirty times. Remember, as Dr. Maoshing Ni would say, "Your stomach does not have teeth!"[79]

question

58 How can I optimize enzyme activity of foods I prepare?

When you select your food at the market, you are bringing home food that was killed once. That's right, that hamburger, chicken, veal, or ham was killed before it made its way to the market. And the longer that meat stayed at the market, the more nutrients were lost. The same holds true for produce. Now, you bring it home and zap it in the microwave, which can virtually wipe out the rest of the life-giving enzymes and nutrients, or you fry your food, which will give you trans fat–laden foods that will not nourish you because they are too busy clogging your arteries! Maybe you are someone who likes to grill your foods. It is now known that eating meat that is charred or blackened may increase your risk of cancer. Now, your food has been killed twice. So how can you prepare your food to best maintain its life-giving properties?

answer

There is evidence to show that the more food is cooked, the more difficult it is to digest and metabolize. This is true of any food. The higher the temperature at which food is cooked, the longer it stays in the gut and the more difficult it becomes for our digestive mechanisms to digest it. This makes it more difficult for the food to be absorbed and to function at a cellular level where it needs to work. When the food cannot function in the cells, the cells become deficient and/or toxic, which leads to deficiency and toxicity of the entire body, making it less able to function optimally.

There are epidemiologic studies that suggest there is a relationship between methods of cooking and various cancers and heart disease. In one study, researchers found that those who ate their beef medium well or well done had more than three times the risk of stomach cancer than those who ate their beef rare or medium rare. Additional studies have shown that an increased risk of developing pancreatic, colorectal, and breast cancer is associated with high intakes of well-done, fried, or barbequed meats.[80]

In other words, you are killing your food twice! The whole point of eating is to remember that the fresher the food and the lighter the preparation, the more nutrition you will receive that will help energize your body and extend your life!

Remember, the body has a difficult time digesting fried, barbecued, overprocessed, and overcooked foods. The more food you can eat raw, the better!

Food preparation tips:

▶ Eat foods that are prepared using low-heat cooking methods that employ water or liquid, like poaching, stewing, braising, boiling, steaming, and slow cooker cooking.

▶ Avoid broiling, frying, hot oven roasting, grilling, and barbecuing.

life-extender tip

Lightly steam, broil, or stir-fry your foods to preserve life-extending nutrients!

A healthy liver is vital to life extension. Your liver is the filter that literally keeps your engine running smoothly. Every system of your body depends on your liver's vitality. Your liver has remarkable regenerative powers. So, if you have consumed too much alcohol, sugar-laden foods, too much animal protein, drugs, or low-fiber diets, there is still time to turn things around and give your liver some TLC. It will repay you with many years of service!

answer

Signs that your liver is in need of assistance include poor digestion, tiredness, weight gain, depression, food and chemical sensitivities, nausea, dizziness, jaundiced skin, skin itching, and congestion. Since your liver's major endeavor is detoxification, if you are experiencing any of the symptoms of poor liver function, I recommend that you take the steps necessary to support the health of your liver right away. It governs your body's ability to metabolize important chemicals such as dopamine, epinephrine, norepinephrine, and sex hormones that can affect your mood and attitude. Undertake a mild detox to lighten your liver's workload so it can focus its energy on rejuvenating and cleansing your system. To detox, just eat a predominately vegetarian diet with emphasis on raw, organic salads and veggies, whole grains, and legumes. Eggs and soft-textured fish such as salmon are also permitted. Avoid fatty or processed foods, refined white flour and sugar, alcohol, caffeine, and nonessential medications. Drink dandelion, peppermint, or chamomile tea and mineral water. Make sure that your last meal of the day is your lightest so that your liver can spend the night rejuvenating instead of detoxifying food by-products. The longer you follow this light detox-eating plan, the lighter you and your liver will feel!

Here is your natural protocol for liver support:

▶ Exercise daily. Your liver is dependent on high-quality oxygen coming into the lungs.

▶ Drink eight to ten glasses of water daily. Add fresh lemon for extra cleansing benefits.

▶ Keep fats low in your diet.

▶ Detoxify your body during the spring and fall seasons of the year using a total body herbal cleanse formula.

▶ Avoid acid-forming foods—red meat, caffeine, alcohol, dairy products, and fried foods.

▶ Increase potassium-rich foods like seafood and dried fruits.

▶ Increase chlorophyll-rich foods like leafy greens.

▶ Increase sulfur-rich foods like eggs, garlic, and onions.

Love your liver by taking:

▶ CoQ$_{10}$
▶ Vitamin C
▶ Milk thistle extract
▶ Dandelion root extract
▶ Artichoke capsules
▶ Acidophilus culture (probiotics)
▶ Royal jelly
▶ Alpha lipoic acid

life-extender tip

Take steps today to care for your liver. A healthy liver makes you a long lifer!

60 What can I do to prevent or reduce inflammation in my body?

We are on the verge of a medical breakthrough. A reversible culprit has been identified that is involved in the development of age-related diseases. That culprit is systemic inflammation. The role of systemic inflammation has been overlooked by the medical establishment, yet scientific evidence exists that correcting a chronic inflammatory disorder will enable many of the diseases of aging to be prevented or even reversed. Inflammation has now been linked to all degenerative diseases, cancer, heart disease, Alzheimer's, and more. It is linked to the most chronic diseases such as asthma, allergies, diabetes, diseases of the skin and bowels, and rheumatoid arthritis. It is important to take steps to reduce your body's level of inflammation.

answer

By the time we reach forty, most of us are battling inflammation in our bodies. It would be good to have your CRP (C-reactive protein) level tested by your doctor to get a clear picture of your status at your next physical. It is a new blood test that is a marker for inflammation in your body. Most insurance plans cover up to twenty dollars of this thirty-dollar test. Recent research shows that people with CRP levels above 3 mg per liter have twice the risk of having a heart attack as people with high cholesterol. In fact, chronic inflammation increases your risk even if you have low or normal cholesterol.

Inflammation softens the plaque buildup that occurs in your arteries as you age. The softened plaque swells and then may burst, choking off blood flow and causing a heart attack. Because CRP testing detects inflammation years before it becomes a serious threat, federal health officials are considering recommending screening so people can take steps to reverse the problem.

Inactivity, obesity, and smoking promote inflammation, so experts agree that the best ways to reverse it are to exercise regularly, slim down, and quit smoking.

Scientists have identified dietary supplements and prescription drugs that can reduce levels of the proinflammatory cytokines (destructive cell signaling chemicals). Fish oil is the best-documented supplement to suppress inflammation. Other supplements are DHEA, vitamin K, GLA (gamma linoleic acid), and nettle leaf. Antioxidants like vitamin E may also lower proinflammatory cytokines.

Dietary changes to reduce CRP levels:

▶ Cut back on refined carbohydrates (sugar, white bread, and white rice) and high-glycemic foods like white potatoes. People who eat diets high in refined or high-glycemic carbohydrates have higher CRP levels.

▶ Take 400 IU of natural vitamin E (d alpha tocopherol) daily. Vitamin E reduces CRP levels.

▶ Eat at least three servings of cold-water fish a week. Or take fish oil capsules daily (1,000 mg). The omega-3 fatty acids found in fish and fish oil lower CRP levels.

life-extender tip

Knock down the "fire within" with nature's anti-inflammatory agents!

61

How I can lift my spirits without resorting to medication?

It is now known that being surrounded by loving friends, family, and associates who are loving and uplifting will provide you with unconditional support and dedication to your well-being, which will in turn benefit your life. Conversely, if you find yourself surrounded by "negative Neds," as I call them, you need to free yourself from these emotional drains and dream wreckers. We all have at least one or two "negative Neds" our lives. They can literally zap your energy and depress your life, destroying your confidence and self-esteem along the way. Free yourself and watch your energy return!

answer

Friendship ranks right up there with laughter when it comes to being medicine for your psyche. An entire new wave of studies shows the power and benefits of social connections. Positive relationships are crucial for your mental and physical well-being, and the absence of these life-enhancing relationships is very detrimental. Researchers are learning that the ties that bind are also the bonds that heal.

It was Abraham Lincoln who said, "The better part of one's life consists of his friendships." New research is showing that women's immune systems suffer from a lack of connection, and men's cardiovascular systems are affected by the lack of a close confidant. Loneliness can be lethal. The lack of positive social relationships can be a health hazard that encourages smoking and drinking and contributes to high blood pressure, lack of exercise, and depression.

Grief and social isolation can lead to weakened immune function, increased risk of cancer, and early death. People with the lowest amount of social ties are two to three times more likely to die of all causes than those with the most social connectedness.[81]

These days with divorce so common and job jumping as a way of life, strong community involvement is lacking, and an epidemic of isolation has emerged.

A friendship is a "heart connection" that literally makes your heart sing and your physical health strong. It is one of the most powerful connections you can make in this life. Friends are flowers in the garden of life. Water them and nurture them with loving care!

Friendships can:

▶ Boost immunity
▶ Prevent depression
▶ Contribute to a longer, happier life

life-extender tip

Take the necessary steps today to fellowship with the healthy, positive, uplifting people in your world!

62 Is it true that love can boost my immune system?

Love is the most powerful emotion in the universe. Many studies have shown that while you are feeling it, your body produces endorphins and immune cells in large numbers. The power of love can heal us of dangerous emotions that threaten to destroy our lives and our health. Why not choose love and live life to the fullest?

answer

When you let go of emotions that are holding you back from vibrant health and abundant life, you will then be able to experience pure love. It will then be possible for you to receive and give love without fear. You will experience a peaceful trust that will replace the mistrust that has held you captive in the past. You will feel more relaxed and at peace in your relationships with your friends and loved ones. Once you are free to accept and give love, you will begin to allow this love to flow out of you and into the lives of everyone and everything you come into contact with. In other words, you will thrive mentally, physically, and spiritually when you develop a lifestyle of loving people unconditionally. Everyone desires love and needs to be loved. You will be amazed at the transformation that takes place in your life. People will be drawn to you. It is a magnet. Love is the universal language. It is a healing balm.

> Love is patient, love is kind, and is not jealous; love does not brag and is not arrogant, does not act unbecomingly; it does not seek its own, is not provoked, does not take into account a

wrong suffered, does not rejoice in unrighteousness, but rejoices with the truth; bears all things, believes all things, hopes all things endures all things. Love never fails.

—1 Corinthians 13:4–8, NAS

Every day is a new beginning, another chance to live in forgiveness, unconditional love, and truth. You must learn to love yourself unconditionally, forgive yourself, and go forth in truth. Be true to yourself. Your body, mind, and spirit will recognize and respond to it! Love yourself as well as your neighbor, unconditionally, and watch how your life will change!

Turn up the love to:

▶ Benefit immunity
▶ Heal your past
▶ Be set free

life-extender tip

Increase your levels of immunoglobulin IGA, which boosts your immunity, by watching a movie about love or romance! Practice loving unconditionally, and learn how to accept love from others.

question

63 Will my efforts to keep my family happy help us live longer?

People with happy family lives tend to have less illness, depression, anxiety, and a longer life span. But what makes a family happy and healthy? There are at least six distinguishing traits that are commonly found in the majority of healthy, happy families. I believe that the more of the following traits your family has, the happier and healthier and more productive your family will be!

answer

Appreciation: Strong and happy families focus on the strengths of each other, not the faults. You can begin today by telling each one of your family members something about them that you love and appreciate. Or just tell them, "I love you because…" Or "I am so proud of you because…"

Commitment: This is *the* most important trait in happy families: commitment to the family—putting the family first—and commitment to each individual in the family in helping him or her overcome and become everything he or she can be. This is a win-win prospect for the entire family because the joy experienced from extending help and support to another family member is equal to the joy, benefit, and support the receiving family member experiences.

Time: Happy and healthy families work, play, and enjoy leisure times together. While they may be busy with jobs, schools, and personal hobbies, they do not let these things steal family time. Schedule time in your appointment book for your family. It is the most important appointment you will ever keep!

Communication: It has been said that the amount of quality time spent in conversation with family members only amounts to about ten minutes per week. To really understand each other, a family has to invest time in talking and listening to each other. Otherwise, even family members can become strangers in this fast-paced world.

Religion: It has been shown that families who share a religious faith and have similar values and standards are happier due to the fact that worshiping together is a bonding experience.

Common interests and goals: The more that family members have in common, the more they want to do things involving each other. A vacation is a great example. Often, the experience of planning the event together is almost as enjoyable as the trip itself!

A happy family makes a healthy family. Leave a legacy of health and happiness, a priceless inheritance for future generations!

Happy families:

▶ Communicate
▶ Appreciate
▶ Commit
▶ Take time
▶ Worship
▶ Share interests

life-extender tip

Today, make an effort to show your family love, respect, help, trust, peace, and sharing.

64 How do I begin to love myself so that I can love others?

To truly love others, you must learn how to love yourself. This is not a selfish thing to do. It is really selfless, for once you learn to love yourself and all of your wonderful God-given attributes, you will then be able to extend that love more deeply and completely to your family, friends, and life partner. But how do you begin to "love yourself" when, in our society, it is often taught that we should deny our own needs and feelings and instead take care of others? And how do we do it when we are often sent messages that we should not accept and love ourselves? This is often true for persons who have survived abuse, whether physical, sexual, or emotional.

answer

The answer is to increase your "self love" in what I call "four little love bytes" or increments.

1. Make a list of all the things you like about yourself, and be honest. This is a time to get real and experience real love. This may be difficult at first since we are taught from childhood to be "modest" or "humble." If you have trouble finding things about yourself that you like, start the process by listing the qualities of your friends that you admire. Could it be that you too possess those same qualities? Like often attracts like!

2. Love yourself as a friend. You know the feeling you have for a trusted friend or lover. It is a feeling that cannot be measured. It creates all kinds of "feel-good" healing chemicals in your body. Now, why not take that feeling and turn it around the other way and be

a friend to yourself? Allow yourself to feel that same deep love for *you*. See yourself through the gentle eyes of love and compassion. If only for a moment, let yourself receive that wonderful feeling of love and acceptance. Revisit this warm feeling each day.

3. Have compassion for yourself. Are you hearing voices of judgment from the past? Where are they coming from? The past is over! What would you tell your children if they felt condemned over something they did in the past? You would probably hug them and tell them that they did not do anything wrong or that it's OK. Then you would tell them that you love them. Why not try to feel that same compassion for yourself?

4. Celebrate *you*! This is a healing thing to do! It nourishes your self-worth. The more you love and appreciate yourself, the happier and more true to your own self you will be. This will ultimately translate into your ability to extend that happiness and love to others.

As you put these four love bytes into practice, remember that above all *you* are a lovable person and *you* deserve lovable treatment. It first must come from *you*!

Love yourself as your neighbor to:

▶ Heal your life
▶ Experience less stress
▶ Enjoy life to the fullest

life-extender tip

Choose an activity that makes you happy—one that shows love to yourself!

65   Why should I forgive?

Unforgiveness is often the result of having a wounded spirit. Someone has forsaken you or betrayed you, or maybe your spouse has committed adultery against you or otherwise emotionally or physically hurt you. Because you are human, you have a tendency to want to "lick your wounds" or even hurt the offender by making sure that he or she knows your condition. One sure thing about harboring unforgiveness in your heart is that you are ultimately the loser.

answer

Forgiveness is a primary key to overcoming dangerous emotions that can destroy your life. Forgiveness is not only good for your mind, but it also provides benefits for your body and soul. A study out of the University of Tennessee tracked subjects' blood pressure and heart rate as they discussed being betrayed by a parent, friend, or lover. As the interviews began, blood pressure shot up for all of the participants. But the levels for those who forgave soon returned to normal. The readings for subjects who were grudge holders stayed high. Interestingly enough, women were more likely to be unforgiving than men.[82]

Most of us want to make sure that things are "even" before we forgive. The truth is, most offenses against us cannot be made right. That's why giving the gift of forgiveness is often the best choice we can make for our health and even the health of the "offender." Many of us are "renting space" in our heads to the painful emotion of unforgiveness. Keep in mind that forgiveness is not admitting someone else is right;

it is letting go of being their judge and jury and giving that job to God. It has been said that unforgiveness is like taking a bitter poison and hoping the other person dies.

Forgiveness is a decision you ultimately have to make. You must consciously choose to give up your feelings of unforgiveness and anger. While anger and resentment are perfectly natural responses to situations that hurt or upset you, you cannot run the risk of letting negative experiences affect your attitude about people or life in general. If you do, it will leave you open to emotional health robbers such as anxiety, depression, poor self-esteem, and remaining in the "victim" role.

If you are dealing with unforgiveness, I encourage you to let go and forgive in order to really live! Holding on to grudges and hurts can sicken your heart, shrivel your soul, and destroy your body. I recommend that you remember what the apostle Paul advised in Ephesians 4:32: "And be kind to one another, tenderhearted, forgiving one another, even as God in Christ forgave you" (NKJV).

Extending forgiveness can:

▶ Improve your mental health
▶ Improve immunity
▶ Help prevent heart disease and high blood pressure
▶ Set you free

life-extender tip

By forgiving, you can move forward without the emotional baggage that prevents you from experiencing an enriched and satisfying life! Forgive one person today and then forget—for good!

question

66 Could the emotions
I am harboring bury me
someday?

Burying something that has caused you emotional pain and
turmoil can ultimately bury you! The best way to neutralize any
negative feelings and regain your self-respect is to acknowledge
your feelings and make them known to others. By doing this you
are cutting off the cascade of life-destroying stress hormones
that can actually shorten our lives.

answer

There is a heavy price to pay when feelings are denied or
repressed. Lethargy, boredom, and a lack of enthusiasm
toward life may be the consequences. Those who are unac-
customed to dealing with feelings in healthy ways often
seek out other means to cover up those feelings or distract
themselves, such as alcohol, food, drugs, TV, unhealthy relationships, or compulsive work.

People who freely express negative emotions may live longer
after heart attacks. A Belgian study of three hundred heart
attack survivors found that those who held in their negative
emotions, particularly anger and fear, were four times more
likely to die within six to ten years after their heart attacks
than a group of survivors who spoke more freely.[83]

Researchers speculate that the emotionally unexpressive
types experience greater stress, which causes spasms in their
arteries and increases the tendency of blood to clot—both of
which contribute to heart problems.[84]

You must "befriend" your emotional self. Start by accepting your emotions as valuable signals that tell you something is in need of attention. Do not try to "chase" your emotions away. Examine them. Express them when it is appropriate to do so. Then MOVE ON!

Wellness is realized by respecting and unburdening yourself of all those things that prevent the natural state of healthiness from being present in your life. To become free is to appreciate simplicity once again. This begins with learning to experience personal peace. Once you discard all of your buried "stuff," you must focus on a higher level of understanding of yourself and others.

Achieve personal peace by quieting your mind and spirit. Learn to love and be loved unconditionally, express gratitude for your life, forgive yourself and others for past transgressions or perceived failures, and let go of resentment and anger. In other words, forgive, trust, and live!

Unearth and discard your repressed hurts so you can:

▶ Prevent health problems
▶ Experience personal peace
▶ Regain your self-respect

life-extender tip

Today, if you feel unhappy, disappointed, or hurt by someone, let them know it. Make peace with them!

67 Why do some people recover from loss faster than others?

How do *you* react during times of stress? Do you react with anger, anxiety, insomnia, avoidance behavior, or fear? There are many documented cases about families that have gone through extremely stressful events. Why do they find that some family members emerged unscathed, while others developed anxiety disorders, health problems, and inability to "let go" of the trauma? The answer is that the family members who fared better after the event learned to "reframe" their perspective on the incident. They did not dwell on it and realized once the event was over, it was over.

answer

Let's go deeper. The key here is to become "emotionally resilient," viewing crises as opportunities for problem solving or as challenges—not as threats to survival. So, just how do you learn to become emotionally resilient?

Emotional resilience doesn't come naturally. Here are six tips I call "healthy you cues" that will get you started on your road to resilience!

1. Learn more productive ways to respond to your problems. Ask yourself, "How does this situation challenge me, and how can I learn from it?"
2. Take care of you. When you are under severe emotional stress, you tend to neglect your own healthy habits. Make sure to always eat a balanced diet, get plenty of sleep, and don't forget to exercise!
3. Observe your stress response. Do you blame yourself? Do you "catastrophize"? Do you believe that nothing

you do will make a difference? Just observing your responses is the starting point on the road to becoming more resilient.

4. Feed your soul. Do something every day that you find deeply pleasurable—walking in the park, listening to your favorite music, or spending time with a trusted friend.

5. Find social support. Sharing your problems with others is a great stress buster. If you find that you are at a loss when it comes to friends or family members who may be willing to listen, there are plenty of support groups out there that focus on just about every problem that you may face in life. Remember that your pastor or church care group is also there to give guidance during life's difficult seasons.

6. Practice gratitude. Take time out each day to focus on things you are grateful for.

By implementing these "healthy you cues" on a daily basis, you will be able to stay centered, even when dealing with a serious illness, financial setback, or other problems that would have derailed you in the past!

Overcome life's curveballs by:

▶ Becoming emotionally resilient

▶ Freeing yourself from self-pity and blame

▶ Forgiving others

▶ Taking time to do something that will lift your spirit

▶ Talking to a good friend or a counselor

▶ Staying healthy by eating right, exercising, and minimizing stress

life-extender tip

Pay attention today when you are under stress. It is how you react rather than how you act that will determine if stress will affect your day and ultimately your health.

What can I do to get my "touch quota" met each day?

Just as orphaned babies stop growing and thriving due to the lack of touch, we adults on some level do not thrive as well when our lives lack touch. Touching promotes elevated production of endorphins, DHEA, and growth hormone. The good news is that this can easily be achieved by hugging someone you love each day. Hugs can lower the levels of stress hormones in your body and lengthen your life span!

answer

Touching can make your immune system stronger and your mood lighter. Touching is a necessity for a healthy life. When we touch, be it a hug, pat, or massage, we receive many health benefits. A half-hour massage can boost your immune system and lessen stress, making you feel calm and happier.

Women especially respond to touch because their skin is more sensitive than a man's. Since women experience higher levels of stress and lower levels of the chemicals that combat stress, a woman's benefit of physical touch is powerful and necessary.

How do you incorporate more touch into your life?

▶ Kiss a friend hello on the cheek. Or give them a quick "hello" hug. These are quick antistress remedies.

▶ Consider buying a pet. Persons who give and receive love to and from their pets can satisfy their daily touch quota. Pets are often used in nursing homes to bring comfort to residents.

▶ Snuggle with your children while watching television. Tackle them for fun, and even give them a back rub. Touching your child can help them develop into loving, caring, and expressive adults.

▶ Rub your partner's back and neck for thirty minutes, then "turnabout" is fair play.

▶ After a long, steamy shower, get out your favorite aromatic lotion and give yourself a massage.

Today's society has developed a "hands off" mentality. The skin that our Creator gave us is the largest sense organ in our bodies and responds positively to every loving touch.

Do you have someone whom you can turn to for a soothing word or gentle touch? If not, one of the best ways is to enjoy textures around you. Velvety pillows, silky clothes, and smooth grass are all sensations we experience through the sense of touch. Have you taken the time to surround yourself with things you like to feel? Let everything you touch in your environment touch you! Take time today to explore creative ways to make your environment a more "touching" place to be.

Touch can:

▶ Increase production of endorphins, DHEA, and growth hormone

▶ Lower the levels of stress hormones in your body

▶ Lengthen your life span

▶ Make your immune system stronger

▶ Lighten your mood and lessen your stress

life-extender tip

Find a hand to hold in this garden of life! Reach out and touch someone you care about today. It has healing benefits for both of you!

69

How do I begin living a more authentic life?

Are you someone who has the "disease to please"? If so, you are not living an authentic life. This can lead to the unhealthiest of all emotions—resentment and anger. When you are true to yourself, you will not feel overwhelmed and overstressed, and you will regain and reclaim control over your life. Living with this "disease" requires you to hand over all of your power to someone else and to surrender your authenticity in search of the great nod of approval. Your only goal becomes getting acceptance and love from anyone and everything outside of yourself. You become so tuned in to other people that you forget the sound of your own melody.

answer

In childhood, the disease to please causes us to turn against our precious and true identity in search of the praise and adoration from our parents. It spreads like a weed through our teenage years as we long to fit in and be accepted by our peers. Then, in adulthood, we are totally consumed, becoming "approval-seeking missiles." When we do not get this approval, we crumble by giving up our self-esteem, boundaries, and self-worth. We lose sight of our own thoughts and opinions; we are so certain that others know better than us that we lift them up onto pedestals of our own creation, only to watch ourselves sink lower into the abyss of self-doubt and despair.

Life was not meant to be lived this way. Eventually we hit rock bottom and realize that if we do not start the healing process, we may lose ourselves forever, buried under layers and years of what others wanted us to be. Shakespeare was aware of this danger when he said, "This above all, to thine own self be true." Unless you reclaim your authentic self, you will be alive and yet not truly live!

How do find your way back to authenticity? You must first take a stand and begin by reclaiming your identity. Start by turning away from living to please others; assert your needs and yourself more when it comes to dealing with people who have exercised control over your life. Our Creator did not make us to be molded by anyone's hands but His.

Slowly you will begin to feel lighter and freer as you drop the desire to please others and get reacquainted with and honor your true nature. You will no longer live as the good soldier marching off to someone else's war.

As we live with authenticity:

▶ We reclaim our freedom.
▶ We take back our power that we gave to others.
▶ We no longer need approval.
▶ We become whole again.

life-extender tip
Today, say what you really mean. If want to say yes to a request, do it! If not, say no!

question

70 What can I do to add joy to my days?

It is now known that many people who have had a coronary event were suffering depression in the weeks, months, or years preceding the event. Research shows that men who feel hopeless have a higher incidence of hypertension. Women who perceive their life to be out of control have a higher incidence of sleeplessness, poor stress responses, and increased risk factors for heart disease and diabetes. Assertively putting joy and happiness into each day is truly a "heart-saving" move!

answer

Stress is an integral part of daily life that allows us to hone our coping skills, but joy is the highest expression of happiness and is essential to healthy living. You need a balance of both stress and joy to live life to the fullest.[85]

How do you incorporate more joy into your life? First of all, take inventory of your "joy account."

▶ What do you love? And are you doing what you love each day?

▶ Whom do you love? Are you spending enough time with those you love?

▶ Do you surround yourself with the people, pets, and things that bring you joy?

▶ Do you have laughter in your daily life?

▶ Do you take yourself or the world too seriously?

To become more joyful, you must realize that the only moment you have is now. Learn to be present in it. Breathe and experience the joy of being alive! Gently and purposely release anything or anyone who no longer adds to or supports your health and happiness. Start to practice respectful distancing and self-care, and set healthy boundaries. Then make your lifestyle choices with love, laughter, and joy with your healthy heart well-being in mind.

Finally—worry and anxiety often stand between us and real joy. I offer you this from Philippians 4:6–7: "Do not be anxious about anything, but in everything, by prayer and petition, with thanksgiving, present your requests to God. And the peace of God, which transcends all understanding, will guard your *hearts* and your minds in Christ Jesus" (NIV, emphasis added).

When you put these principles into practice, the natural result will be to attract more joy into your life. You will literally magnetize it. Live life with all of your heart!

Add joy to your life by:

▶ Doing one thing you love to do every day
▶ Spending time with good friends
▶ Watching a funny movie
▶ Playing with your children or grandchildren
▶ Getting a pet
▶ Releasing your worries to God
▶ Living in the now

life-extender tip

Do one thing today that brings you joy! Remember the joy of your youth, and recapture that euphoric feeling of happiness!

71

Where can I find someone to share my innermost feelings?

Today, identify who your support person is. Is it a trusted friend, family member, or co-worker? By sharing your innermost feelings with a "safe" listening partner, you will be able to release your burdens and at the same time deepen your relationship with that person. By trusting them with your concerns, you build intimacy. Someday that very same support person may just need your support too! Whom will they turn to? YOU!

answer

According to James S. House of the University of Michigan, data indicate that social isolation is as significant to mortality as high blood pressure, smoking, high cholesterol, obesity, and lack of physical exercise. A study by the University of California at Berkeley found that "adults who did not cultivate nurturing relationships, refusing to even own a pet, have premature death rates twice as high as those with frequent, caring contact."[86]

Dr. James House reviewed an extensive body of literature in the 1980s that studied a total of ten thousand women. The conclusion was that social isolation increases your risk of dying from all causes.[87]

A small town in Rosetta, Pennsylvania, that is known for being one of the healthiest communities in the country was investigated to determine just why its residents enjoy such good health. It was discovered that the residents were very close knit. People knew one another and frequently had dinners together. When a resident was in trouble, the community rallied to help see them through. This community's mutual support was way above the norm.

Science now proves that having a good support system, which includes deep, personal friendships, can be very beneficial to your health. As Winnie the Pooh so wonderfully said, "You can never have too many friends or too much honey!"

How do you insure closer interpersonal relationships?

▶ Family: Create a family night each week or spend personal time with each family member this week.

▶ Friends: Nurture your quality friendships. Dedicate special time for others.

▶ Neighbors: Be friendly and attentive to those who live near you.

▶ Organizations: Join a local organization in which you can share your skills and develop new friendships.

▶ Work: Do not neglect valuable relationships with your co-workers.

▶ Church: A church family can easily become the core of your personal support system. Become involved. Helping others is one of the best ways to boost your health!

life-extender tip

Feeling anxious today? Talk it out with a trusted friend!

How do I take responsibility for my own health?

Taking responsibility for your health may seem like something you pay your doctor to do, but the first step in living a long, healthy, and fulfilling life is to recognize that *you* are responsible for making *your* health *your* business! It is *not* up to your doctor! When you take responsibility for doing all of the things in life that keep you well, you will have a much greater chance of staying healthy and living longer. To be responsible for you is empowering!

answer

When we make choices, we are taking responsibility and exerting a degree of control. This is a major determinant in how disease progresses. When exposed to adversity, even laboratory animals that are able to make a choice to stop the stress are far less likely to suffer from disease compared with the animals that are helpless.[88] The same is true of people. Sometimes circumstances may leave little in your control. But you can always decide what you will focus on and the attitude you adopt toward it.

Choice is your greatest asset and a very precious gift. It is empowering, especially when it comes to your health!

To experience health, you must deliberately choose to adopt a healthy lifestyle:

▶ Take time to rest. Rest will give you peace and will refresh you mentally and physically.

- Create a healthy environment for yourself. De-clutter your life.

- Determine to be physically active. Get plenty of fresh air. Go for a walk!

- Cultivate interpersonal relationships. Give hugs and plenty of smiles! Spend quality time with those you care about.

- Check your outlook. Take inventory of yourself mentally and emotionally. Seek aid and support from those who care and are skilled in helping people overcome anxiety and/or depression, if necessary.

- Eat healthfully and drink plenty of water. Your body will quickly let you know how much it likes your healthy choices by supplying you with more energy!

- Trust. Your trust in God speaks to the important relationship between spirituality and healing. Your faith, beliefs, and hopes all affect your health.

Each positive health choice you make only makes the next healthy step easier. And so it goes, onward and upward to living life at its best!

Taking responsibility for your health includes:

- Making good food and nutritional choices
- Exercising
- Getting enough sleep
- Going for regular health checkups
- Maintaining balance in your life

life-extender tip

This day, choose to "put your hands back on the wheel" of your health! Kenneth Patton once said, "By the choices and acts of our lives, we create the person that we are."[89]

What can I do to help myself become a more patient person?

Patience is a virtue. Did you know that having patience will also safeguard you from the frustration, anger, anxiety, and depression of trying to make things happen according to *your* plan? You will probably realize that things unfolded just fine anyway, and all of that wasted energy spent on trying to "swim upstream" just left you exhausted, stressed, and depleted. Let go! Trust! Be patient, or maybe someday you will *be* a patient!

answer

Patience is truly a foreign concept to many of us in this "microwave" generation. But there is no quick fix for the angst of impatience. Circumstances and people can sometimes push us over the edge and try even the patience of Job!

When faced with a trying situation and your patience is "wearing thin," simply detach inwardly from the problem and see it for what it really is. Read about the subject and pay attention to how others have overcome it. Become a problem solver, not a problem creator.

Learning to be patient allows a lot of space for the other person involved to speak and to express themselves while you do not react, even though inside you are reacting. Being patient means letting go and just being there. Keep in mind that this does not mean you suppress any anger or dissatisfaction you may be feeling; patience has nothing to do with suppression. It instead has everything to do with a gentle, open, and honest relationship with yourself. If a situation is too big and you can't seem to let it go, just practice little ways to slowly release it. Once you begin to feel the relief and relaxation that come from it, you will see that holding on to the situation only increases your pain. Letting go stops it!

How to live patiently:

▶ Pray. When you come to the end of yourself in a trying situation, prayer will help you enter a higher dimension where you can welcome help from above.

▶ Laugh. While waiting, laughter fills your heart and lessens the load that the "wait" has caused.

▶ Be thankful! The attitude of gratitude applies here. Let your thanksgiving exceed your complaining.

▶ Love the people involved unconditionally. This may seem like a tough one, but no one is beyond redemption.

▶ Be at peace. Practice letting peace reign in your own heart and mind as you patiently wait for an outcome. Agitations will be lessened and brought into perspective, and the atmosphere around you will be peaceful.

life-extender tip

Are you impatient? Let life "open its door" to you rather than you trying to "kick" it open by forcing your own timetable upon it. Trust that everything happens at just the right time. It does!

74

How can I free myself of words that cut so deep so long ago?

As children we used to say, "Sticks and stones may break my bones, but names will never hurt me." But as we grew into adulthood, we realized that we probably would rather have had a broken bone or two than to be called a name that hurt us to the core and then got stuck there. We realize that those words actually began to grow into many of the limitations we place on our adult selves. Memories of "you're too fat, too thin, too dumb, too lazy, not good enough" plague many of us even though none of these things have any basis in our reality. Words are powerful, so powerful, in fact, that what you tell yourself about you can set the stage for failure or success, sickness or health, happiness or despair. What you speak, you *will* have. Keep in mind that what you speak to others leaves a lasting impression. So choose all of your words wisely. They have a very deep impact on you!

answer

Too often, when bad things happen to us and we are in pain, we want to blame someone or make someone else hurt. This is when your words can cut like a knife, and the wound, though invisible, leaves lasting pain that often never heals. Controlling the tongue means stopping the blame game and starting to take responsibility for your own emotions and behaviors.

There are three main "tongue ties" that will help you control the words that stick like barbs into the hearts of those you love and care about:

1. *Look for the good.* Choose today to focus your thoughts on the good traits of people and conditions. It is not that you do not see or accept the bad, but rather, you choose to turn your thoughts toward goodness.
2. *Forgive.* Do not dwell on the past! Let go of being another person's judge and jury.
3. *Take responsibility.* Own your own stuff when it comes to your situation. What kind of attitude have you been toting around? Does your point of view need some adjustments? Do an "internal inventory."

It has been said that life and death are in the power of the tongue. Why not make it a habit to speak life to all you come into contact with? Why tear down when you can build up? Why wound when you can heal with comforting words? Why destroy yourself in the process?

Guard your tongue by:

▶ Looking for the good in others or in a life situation

▶ Forgiving and releasing hurts from the past

▶ Owning your mistakes gracefully

▶ Giving sincere compliments

▶ Making positive affirmations, such as "I choose love, joy, and freedom, and I open my heart to allow wonderful things to flow in."

life-extender tip

According to the Chinese, most diseases come from things that enter the mouth, and most trouble comes from words that leave it![90] Guard your tongue today; it may ruin someone else's tomorrow!

75

How can I embrace the idea of changing my lifestyle and health?

As you continue on your journey to find answers on how to live longer, I want you to remember why you decided to take this journey. Who were you at the beginning of this trek? Were you tired, wired, anxious, depressed, unfocused, chronically ill, or out of balance? As you apply the principles found on this journey, notice who you are becoming. You should be feeling more empowered and more educated on the subject of *you*! Your outlook should be a positive one, which makes you more willing to take charge of your life, body, mind, and spirit and be more excited at the prospect of living a healthier, more vibrant life!

answer

One of the most positive changes you can make that will help you "become" the very best you is to change your outlook. By adopting a positive outlook you can literally change your life!

There is scientific support that proves your outlook is more than simply a state of mind. It can influence how your brain manages the healing process. Some studies suggest that simply by thinking positive thoughts, you can turn on the side of the brain linked with improved immunity.

Depression is often the result of having a negative outlook and is strongly linked to the destruction of your physical health. Depression alone is now an independent risk factor for heart disease. It may even be as bad as high cholesterol. Heart disease isn't the only illness worsened by depression. Those who suffer from cancer, diabetes, epilepsy, and osteoporosis all appear to run a higher risk of disability or premature death when they are clinically depressed. So it is clear to see that your outlook plays an enormous role in who you are becoming.

Five practical boosters to help ensure your outlook success!

▶ Self-talk: Compliment yourself on every step of your progress toward vibrant health!

▶ Distraction techniques: Rather than allowing yourself to despair, use a distraction technique to give yourself some time and distance so you can choose the best response to the situation.

▶ Shift attention: Simply think about something else. Recall happy memories from years gone by. You will find that it will then be easier to plan what to do next with better perspective and the added benefits of an elevated mood.

▶ Put problems on hold: When negative thoughts race through your mind, make yourself an "appointment" to think about them—later. When you are rested, calm, and clear headed, your responses will be wiser.

▶ Write a letter: When you write down your negative thoughts, they tend to lose their hold on you.

life-extender tip

Today, pay attention to your outlook and the new you that you are becoming!

76 What can I do to stop feeling like a failure?

So many of us have big dreams and hopes of changing the world and making a huge mark in history. We have high expectations of what we hope to accomplish one day, but I am here to tell you that it is not the world that needs to be changed in order for you to make a difference—it is *you*! All of us are going through change every day. Sometimes we have to stop and refocus our ideas about success and failure. Sometimes the desire you have to change something may not be directed at the *whole* world; it may just be that you need to make changes that will improve *your* world. And sometimes your feelings of failure may be related to your health habits.

answer

One way to change your world is to change your environment. Your environment influences your health and can foster peace and well-being.

Are you living in an "Eden environment"? Are your surroundings cheerful and happy? Are they places that nurture your soul and recharge your spirit? Do you feel happy and calm when you are in them? Do they provide you with comfort, offer opportunity for growth, and give you a sense of peace?

Here are five steps to create an Eden environment that will change your world.

1. *Sight:* Add beautiful sights to your personal world. Place fresh flowers on your dinner table, nightstand, or dressing area. Watch a sunset.

2. *Taste:* Eat a variety of colors. Find a farmer's market and buy lots of yellow, red, green, and orange fruits and vegetables. Choose crunchy whole grains and cereals and wake up your taste buds. Enjoy new flavors!

3. *Smell:* Bring fragrance into your life. Vanilla, lavender, cinnamon, and pine all help produce a feeling of well-being. Add a bouquet of fragrant flowers to your bedside table. Buy scented candles that minister to your senses. Use body lotions and creams that soothe your skin and make you feel good.

4. *Touch:* Lead a happier life by using touch each day. Ask for and give appropriate hugs. Have a massage. Pamper yourself. Take a hot bath or shower at the end of a long day. Buy thick, thirsty towels to wrap your body in. Lie down on soft, silky sheets and bedding.

5. *Sound:* Add peaceful sounds to your life. Add a fountain to your backyard, then sit outside and listen to the sound of the flowing water. Buy a songbird. Take time to find the type of music that sings to your soul, and play it when you feel stressed.

Make your environment a "Garden of Eden." Have a little bit of heaven here on earth!

Start feeling like a success by:

▶ Eating healthy and fresh

▶ Getting enough sleep

▶ Seeking balance in *all* areas of your life

▶ Loving more, stressing less

▶ Changing the way you view things

---

life-extender tip

Today, lighten up, let go, live more, and change your environment. Then sit back and watch your world change!

How can I tame the "green-eyed monster" within me?

We are all born with specific gifts, strengths, and attributes. Just like snowflakes, no two individuals are alike. Why then should jealousy exist? It is a wasted emotion that seeks to destroy rather than to build. Jealousy indicates insecurity in your self-worth and lack of confidence in your ability. Jealousy is one of the worst poisons of any relationship. The devastating effects are twofold: first, jealousy ruins good communication between people, causing a multitude of unfounded arguments and fights; and second, jealousy conveys some of the most unattractive qualities, like insecurity, which is one of the biggest turnoffs when it comes to having relationships with others.

answer

Eliminating jealousy is not a quick process because it is a character trait, a frame of mind, and an emotion. Getting rid of it is a gradual process that requires work, patience, persistence, and self-examination.

The good news is that the reward of dealing with, overcoming, and finally getting free of jealousy is to experience life and relationships to the fullest!

Here are simple steps to keep the green-eyed monster at bay:

1. Recognize that you have a problem. This is essential to your motivation to work on it and to your success in overcoming jealousy. Many people who have jealousy issues are in denial of the fact that they do.

2. To remove jealous thoughts from your mind, spend more of your time and your emotional and intellectual resources on building yourself.

3. Work on your career and other goals. Pursuing other objectives of your life will prevent you from obsessing over other people's "stuff."

4. If you are in a relationship and find yourself jealous, remember that the best "leash" is a loose one, or even better, no leash at all. Remember, the only thing that keeps your partner around you is his or her desire to be with *you*! The desire does *not* come from pressure, your being jealous, or your attempts to convince him or her to be faithful to you, but it comes from your other qualities that make you attractive and desirable.

By getting rid of jealousy, you will:

▶ Exhibit a very attractive quality in yourself—confidence

▶ Increase your ability to attract other people, places, and things into your life

▶ Decrease jealousy's destructive, stressful effects on your body, such as high blood pressure and ulcers

▶ Have time to focus on improving yourself

life-extender tip

One of the most destructive emotions is jealousy. The truth is that there is plenty of room for everyone to succeed! Why not celebrate another person's greatness? Call one person you admire today and tell them how much you admire their achievements.

78 How do I slow down this stressful cycle I'm in?

Is your life stressed? Are you often in a hurry? Do you get less than seven hours of sleep a day? Do you find yourself feeling overwhelmed or out of control? Do small things cause you to have big reactions? Do you not give the most important people in your life your undivided attention? What's your hurry? Life is meant to be savored and lived well and long. Living life in the fast lane is a fast track to stress-related disorders, heart disease, and other degenerative diseases.

answer

Today's world has programmed us to pack more and more into each twenty-four-hour day. We phone, fax, e-mail, page, and overnight deliver. At home, our schedules are packed with family activities. Then we "relax" in front of the TV where sixty to six hundred channels all vie for our attention.

Our lives can be way too overloaded. Here are seven tips to help you put the brakes on a life that is moving too fast!

1. *Pray:* Worry and anxiety come between you and your health. When you have had a stressful day or life is dishing up more than you can handle, prayer is a great stress reliever. The peace of God that transcends all understanding will guard your heart.

2. *Sleep:* Develop a regular sleep pattern. Reduce caffeine intake. Try to get eight hours each night. You cannot play "catch up" when it comes to meeting your daily sleep quota. Adopt a relaxing bedtime ritual such as taking a warm bubble bath or listening to soft music.

3. *Take a vacation:* Start planning a real vacation, not just an occasional day off here and there. Take a vacation without cell phones, computers, and other work-related activities. Really get away. Play. Rest.

4. *Breathe:* Proper breathing will help you relax. Breathe slowly and deeply. Start from the bottom of your lungs and breathe slowly through your nose. Count slowly to five while exhaling through tight lips twice as long as you inhaled. Repeat this breathing exercise four or five times until your breathing begins to slow down and become relaxed.

5. *Dream:* Take twenty-second mini vacations daily. This will help resync your mind and reenergize you.

6. *Laugh:* Laughter can help lower blood pressure, relax your muscles, and help your brain release endorphins, which are chemicals that make you feel *good*! Call an old friend and laugh it up!

7. *Rest:* Rest your body, mind, and soul each day.

Slowing down will:

▶ Give you the energy you need to make a priority the things that really count

▶ Add quality and years to your life

▶ Make you more creative and effective in your work and personal life

▶ Allow you to enjoy your successes

life-extender tip

Practice slowing life down today. Those who live fast die young.

question

79

How do I cope with issues beyond my control?

Are you frazzled, wired, and frustrated? It's time to go deep! Just like a submarine when faced with a possible attack, you must dive, dive, dive! Dive deeply into your core. "Be still, and know that I am God" (Ps. 46:10, NKJV). In that stillness, you will find your center again. You will find solid ground. When you resurface, you will emerge as if you have been given respite. The world that you want to live in will not emerge instantly for you, but rather, it will only emerge from a stillness that takes root in your soul. The only way to escape the outer world that is moving way too fast is to learn to slow down. The only way to spread your influence wide is to go deep.

answer

When your world is troubling and you are dealing with issues that are beyond your control, you do not need to join in the chaos. You need to cleave to the peace that lies deep within you.

Each of us is connected to our Creator by a "spiritual umbilical cord," from which we can still receive daily nourishment every moment. As you take the time to go deep, this nourishment is needed more than ever and will sustain you like never before. This is because maybe for the first time, you are not dining on the "mental junk food" of the world but rather on the divine manna that lies deep within. Who you really are is an issue bigger than all of your problems, both personally and collectively. When you remember who you really are—who God created you to be—your problems, which are just "manifestations of your forgetfulness," will disappear.

As you abandon your desire to drink the poison of this world—mental confusion, fear, competition, anger, hatred, and unforgiveness—even when darkness may seem to be all around you, going deeper will ultimately "light your way home." This is a homecoming to the real you.

A new you will be reborn, a new you in which the wonders of the world are no comparison to what has happened within you. You will be free from the limitations of fear. Faith will reign supreme. Your outer world will now be a reflection of your inner sanctuary.

By going deep, you essentially die to who you once were, and you become instead what God intended you to be! Whole, healed, and—most of all—free!

Dive deep by:

► Slowing down
► Entering spiritual stillness
► Focusing your attention on who you *really* are

life-extender tip

Ignore things that are happening outside of you and are out of your control. Go deep within to find that "stillness" on the inside.

question

80

I recently lost my job.
How do I deal with
this change?

These days, change is occurring at alarming rates—divorces, job losses, aging, careers, and so much more. Change is an inevitable part of life. It is something that many of us fight or are afraid of. I call change a gift because it is *always* an opportunity for personal growth and maturity. Many people will agree that if a particular change did not occur when it did, their lives would not be as rich or as rewarding as they are now.

answer

When I have been faced with change in my own life, I have found that when I remembered who was walking with me, I had the courage to face it. People are often afraid of change. That is because change is a force that causes a shift in your world—ready or not! The key is to move slowly when change is coming at you fast. You must be conscious and prayerful before, during, and after change.

An important thing to remember, when change has occurred in your life, is that time is needed to adjust to the new turn life has taken. You need time to "grow" into your circumstances. You need to inhabit emotionally the new space you may be occupying materially. You need time to think about what this change means and how to deal with it in the most mature way.

Change also forces you to say good-bye to parts of yourself or your life that are being called to be transformed or discarded. Change forces you to say hello to a part of you that is being born. Rushing through change is not advisable. It is a setup for mistakes! Most people would agree that the biggest mistakes they made in life were because they did not take the time to think, meditate, or pray about the situation.

Embracing change through the eyes of love instead of fear will give you the courage to endure or to make changes in your life. Without fear, your perceptions will change. Change should be embraced as a lesson. It is a part of the educational process God constitutes as your next assignment. With every challenge or lesson, you are challenged to go deeper and become wiser and more loving.

The road home is not often a horizontal one but a vertical one. Trust God during every change. He has trusted the change in you and has orchestrated it even before you were born!

To thrive during change:

▶ Remember who is walking with you!
▶ Embrace change through the eyes of love—not fear!
▶ Trust. Think vertically.
▶ Remember, change is a challenge to grow!

life-extender tip

Be open to any change in your life. Embrace it! It is God's challenge to you to grow! Change is a gift. Receive it in that way!

The Quakers have a process known as "centering down." It simply means finding that calm stillness within. It is a restful place where you can feel and go to when life gets out of balance. This could be a place where you can be alone with your thoughts and prayers, a place that is physically beautiful and comforting, a place where you feel safe and secure, a place where you can play uplifting music and spend time in reflection.

answer

We were designed to live in rhythm. We must take time for rest, relaxation, and rejuvenation. God has even placed resting places between each one of your heartbeats. The resting period between each beat allows your heart to reload. And so it goes with our entire being. We must step out of the fast lane, rest, and reload.

Even Eleanor Roosevelt knew the importance of "centering down" when she said, "A day out-of-doors, someone I loved to talk with, a good book and some simple food and music—that would be rest."[91] Sir William Penn also knew the importance of "being still." He said, "True silence is the rest of the mind; it is to the spirit what sleep is to the body, nourishment and refreshment."[92]

Do you lose your concentration often? Do you find that you regularly have to "jump-start" your brain in the morning or afternoon with stimulants such as coffee, sugar, or medication? Is worry, anxiety, or panic a daily occurrence? Do you multitask? Do you overcommit? Are you crisis driven? Are you too emotional? Do you sleep enough? Do you live in a pattern of overwork?

If you answered yes to any of these questions, you must rest and reload! Taking time out to bond with God each day will create a peaceful center in your life. In other words, you will know how to "center down."

Evaluate your life:

► How many of hours of sleep do you get each night?
► How much time each day do you spend with your family?
► How much time do you spend with God each day?

You need to build into each day a "Sabbath" of sorts—a time to stop working, a time to stop making and spending money, a time to see what you really have, a time to look around and listen to your life and begin to think about all of the blessings in your life.

As you center down:

► Close the door of your mind to past hurts and wounds.
► Ask God to heal you of all hurt and pain.
► Look forward to the future with certainty that you are loved.
► Know that each beat of your heart is kept by your Creator.

life-extender tip

Rest, reload, and center down!

question

82

Do you have any advice that will help me purge old habits?

Who are you at this very moment? Each of us has within us the ability for greatness. Narrow is the road that leads there, and the twists and turns are plentiful. Many times it takes sacrificing something of yourself to travel this "higher road." If you choose to take the trip, you really aren't sacrificing but *allowing* your life experience to be raised to a higher level of fulfillment. This takes ridding yourself of old ways, habits, persons, and patterns that have hindered your higher walk with your Creator. Be ready to let go of the old and make room for the new improved you that God had in mind even before you were in your mother's womb!

answer

We all have suitcases packed full of mistakes, injustices, illness, and sadness. It is time to leave that suitcase on the sidewalk of life and walk away from it. We have invested so much of our lives carrying our suitcases that we are often "over the weight limit," remembering the contents, and refusing to say yes to new life that doesn't "match" the old baggage.

Taking the higher road is not always easy; it requires daily acts of adaptation, courage, and love.

As you read this chapter, you are creating your next moment. Everything you think, everything you do, everything you are is predicting who you are becoming. Becoming the best you is living today and creating tomorrow with God's direction and intention.

To give your whole heart over to letting go of the old you requires you to sometimes endure pain, loss, or change. But you will have something worthwhile at the end of the challenge. That is, a life that is more wonderful than anything you can imagine, now lived by a new you—more precious, useful, and talented than you have ever been before. You will discard your old suitcase and open a "treasure chest"! But this time it will be filled with uplifting thoughts, positive people, and wisdom from God! Let go of the old; embrace the new you!

You know you need to drop off your old baggage and buy a new suitcase if you:

▶ Feel like you need to become a better you

▶ Feel hopeless

▶ Find it hard to imagine a satisfying future

▶ Feel overwhelmed

▶ Can't remember your dreams

▶ Want to change something in your life but don't know how

▶ Are often sad

life-extender tip

Be ready, at any moment, to sacrifice what you are for what you could become.

question

83

What can relieve my anxious desire to know the whys of life?

Proverbs 3:5 tells us, "Do not lean on your own understanding" (NAS). Things may not be easily understood, but in the supernatural realm of God, all things are working in divine order. That is the way God designed the universe—all things working in perfect order. Our ways are often not His ways. Our natural minds cannot even begin to perceive the intricacy of our Creator's grand design.

answer

Instead of living in frustration about things in life that are beyond your control, just remember that Jesus said, "I have overcome the world" (John 16:33, NAS). He did not say, "I have fixed the world." When you let go and stop trying to fix things in your life that do not make sense, you will have "overcome" the world. You will have learned to trust that whatever may be happening, there is a plan and a purpose.

You must realize that some problems and difficulties have no answers now. They will, however, have an answer someday, especially if your understanding of God's universe increases. Trusting God for answers will bring you to a place of peace in your heart and mind.

You may never see the beginning from the ending of God's plan for your life, but God sees the big picture and all the details that are a part of it!

Let God untangle situations that have caused you angst and frustration. Every problem in life is not bad. If it's happening, think of it as part of God's divine curriculum where all involved will learn from it.

Life, when lived with the full understanding of God, is not about problems; rather it's about becoming someone who knows how to dwell within problems in a positive way. It is living with the faith that God's miracle is on the way!

From the womb to the tomb, life can be lived with the knowing that God is bigger than any circumstance we endure and any challenge we face. God is bigger than any limitations that our world may be showing us now.

Go beyond logic:

▶ God has a plan for your life.

▶ He is in every detail.

▶ Stop trying to "fix" in order to overcome!

life-extender tip

Today, go beyond logic; the world functions in divine order.

84

What can I do to have peace in my life?

Peace comes to you when you learn and practice contentment in all situations. Whatever you may be facing today, decide to be joyful, patient, and faithful in your prayer life. When dealing with any problem in life, we long for the healing, comforting balm of peace. Peace can only come when faith is applied, and joy only happens when you are at peace. Most persons will tell you that when they realized what their unique purpose was on this earth and began to fulfill it, the result was peace and joy.

answer

To experience real peace, you must live purposely. Once you know your purpose, you need to make a commitment to yourself to live according to that purpose. Let all of your actions and activities reflect your purpose. Living outside of your true purpose will cause frustration, while living purposely will bring you great joy!

Expand your horizons, give more than you take, do the unexpected, indulge yourself frequently, and laugh a lot! Joy can be yours if you look for it, pursue it, and enjoy it.

Richard Foster, author of *Celebration of Discipline*, said, "Joy is the motor that keeps everything else going. It produces energy. It makes us strong."[93]

How are you feeling right now? Are you angry, disappointed, hurt, or harboring unforgiveness? All of these things are roadblocks to true joy. Take time to restore or mend relationships. Right any wrongs. Return to the days of your youth when joy was the norm. Go back to that innocence that once was yours. That is where you first felt joy at its best. Purpose to laugh, play, run, dance, and sing! Psalm 30:5 (NKJV) says, "Joy comes in the morning," but joy can come right now. It is up to you. You can take the steps necessary to restore peace and joy in your life. While joy does not mean that we are never sad or that we never cry, it is a confidence, a state of inner peace that comes from God.

Restoring joy to your life is essential to consistent Christian living. It is required for you to be an authentic witness and will enable you to enjoy a closer walk with God. When your heart is surrendered totally to the will of God, then you can delight in seeing Him use you in any way He pleases. Your plans and desires begin to agree with His, and you accept His direction in your life. Your sense of joy and fulfillment in life will increase, no matter what the circumstances, if you are in the center of God's will!

Peace and joy are found by:

▶ Feeling forgiven

▶ Forgiving others

▶ Living your purpose

▶ Being thankful

▶ Staying in fellowship with God

▶ Giving more than you take

life-extender tip

Today, focus on being "joyful in hope, patient in affliction, and faithful in prayer" (Rom. 12:12, NIV).

85

Can you give me tips on how to be my true self?

Whom do you see when you look in the mirror? Is it someone whom you can be proud of? Are you someone who feels confident in knowing that your life mirrors what you proclaim your core beliefs to be? If not, it is time to get back to the essential you—your authentic self!

answer

▼

Being true to yourself means being consistent with what you say, think, or do. It has nothing to do with saying yes to things in life that are not true to your nature. It means stopping the need to please people and letting the real you shine through. How do you get there? There are four basic steps.

Be true to you by:

1. *Identifying your true nature:* This is the state of being that fuels your passion and gives you an abiding sense of purpose. It is here that you will find your true self. It is who you really are, who God created you to be. It is the you who existed before environmental influences began to shape you, creating patterns of behavior that were not authentic.

2. *Engaging in proactive behavior:* Do things that allow you to get in touch with your true self. Spend time in prayer. Do the things that bring joy to your life. Take care of your needs. Say what you mean. Mean what you say!

3. *Taking action:* Think of yourself as a newborn, a clean slate, if you will. Then picture yourself growing and evolving into maturity—whole, positive, and fearless. As a child of God, this is your true nature. Now,

with this in mind, realize that life can be full of limit-less possibilities if you become true to yourself and embrace them!

4. *Becoming free:* Your new sense of wholeness will free you from the fear of not being good enough. This will cause you to engage in self-affirming behavior. You will be able to make authentic contributions to your-self and the world. In doing so, you will become the full expression of what God intended you to be![94]

Your life is a gift from God. Why not show your gratitude by being who He created you to be?

When you become true to you:

▶ You will be awake to the wonder of living a life without regrets.

▶ You will become more productive and will contribute more to the world than ever before.

▶ The world will finally receive the gift of the real you!

life-extender tip

Today and from now on, strive to make your life consistent with your proclaimed beliefs.

86

How can I learn to be honest without hurting someone?

Today is the day to rid yourself of the "disease to please." Begin today by saying no when you know that you must. Be the most authentic you possible. It is freeing. Let your "yea be yea" and your "nay be nay." Say what you mean. Doing this will help to build a network of friends who are truly friends. Saying yes out of some sort of duty, guilt, or perceived obligation only creates unhealthy, unbalanced relationships. Call your boundaries by saying no when you really want to. It is more than OK to do so. In the end, not only will you gain the respect of others, but also your self-respect will increase!

answer

I know that it is hard to let down friends, neighbors, co-workers, and others who rely on you. Without boundaries, you invite others, and *their* priorities, to take over your life! As a result, you will become frustrated, overwhelmed, and possibly resentful—not a good way to feel about those in your life whom you care about. The answer? It is very simple. The next time someone asks you to "help out," consider what you will be giving up to fulfill the obligation. You must be deliberate in how you use your time. After all, it is *your* time. Learn how to push the guilt aside when saying no.

To help get you started, here is a mini course on how to say no:

► "I'm sorry. I won't be able to."
► "Maybe next time."

- ▶ "I've got plans."
- ▶ "I have a previous engagement."
- ▶ "I have an appointment that I can't break."
- ▶ "I would love to, but I am busy that day."

How to "buy time":

- ▶ "I might have to work."
- ▶ "I need to check my schedule."
- ▶ "Let me check with my husband/wife."
- ▶ "Let me get back to you."

Have a "policy":

- ▶ "I'm sorry. I have a policy: I don't help friends move."
- ▶ "I'm sorry. I have a policy: I don't lend people money."
- ▶ "I'm sorry. I have a policy: I don't dog sit."

(These may sound harsh, but actually people find it a little humorous while still getting the point.)

Saying no will protect you from:

- ▶ Frustration
- ▶ Feelings of being overwhelmed
- ▶ Resentment

life-extender tip

A no uttered from the deepest conviction is better than a yes merely uttered to please.

87 How can I get free from regrets of the past?

Are you haunted by the past? Mistakes made, hurts you may have caused, things left unsaid or undone? Today, know that you have a God of second, third, and fourth chances. God forgives. It is time to once and for all forgive yourself and others in your past. By "cutting the ties that bind" you to the hurt of the past, you are free.

answer

You will never be free to pursue your future until you are free from the past. Just trying to forget the pain doesn't heal it. Unresolved issues can get stuck in the back of your mind and become "tormenting vexations," which is something that consumes. Your past issues will continue to dominate your attention, become the focus of your thoughts, and render you incapable of giving attention to the present because you are so stuck in the past.

Anything that you focus your attention on is made larger in your experience. By focusing on the regrets of your past, you only make those regrets larger in your mind. In other words, you magnify them. As a result it becomes a "vexation," which is just the opposite of worship! As you continually focus on your past and all of its pains, you magnify or grow them large as you focus your attention on them.

We all have heard that we can recover from the past just by forgiving people who have hurt us. However, that is just one part of the recovery. The next important step on the road to recovery is to release people, including yourself, from your judgments. It is an incredible act of kindness toward yourself!

Accept God's forgiveness and experience the release of judgment and pain your past brought you. Burn the "letters of grievance" you have written about yourself. Watch them be consumed by the flames of your forgiving Father's unconditional love. As the smoke rises and dissipates, see your past doing the same thing. Knowing that God has forgiven your past enables you to live free and to discover the wonderful life ahead!

To release your past and experience forgiveness, remember:

▶ Your old self, with all its sins, limitations, and the judgments you passed against it, is dead once you accept the gift of salvation.

▶ God's judgment does not leave you in the grave, so don't put yourself there. He raises you daily into newness of life!

▶ When you release your judgment of yourself and your past, you will see yourself from God's perspective— forgiven, made righteous, and accepted!

▶ You will be free when you believe you are who God says you are!

life-extender tip

Don't let yesterday use too much of today!

88 I *love* to give. Can you ever give too much?

It is true; the best things in life are free—love, joy, peace, friendship, and, most of all, your ability to give. Giving is beneficial to both the giver and recipient. Jesus said, "Give, and it will be given to you" (Luke 6:38, NAS). Giving is the key to more powerful living. Giving is a way to express gratitude for all that you have been given. Giving is as good for the giver as it is for the receiver. Science even says so. You will be happier and healthier, and, odds are, you will live a little longer if you are generous.

answer

Reaching out a hand to lift someone else up is one of the greatest gifts for the heart. The gifts that one receives from giving back and from reaching out to help others are immense and priceless. When you are generous even in small, barely detectable ways, it can change someone's life forever.

By giving some of your time or volunteering to a worthy cause, you will experience true altruism. You will experience what is called a "helper's high" as your levels of endorphins increase!

I must stress, however, that while giving to others has enormous benefits to your mind, body, and spirit, you must not neglect giving to yourself. You cannot give to others what you do not have.

Give yourself the time, love, and undivided attention you so often give to others. Sing, dance, read, cook, sew, run, and swim. Just be!

Take time out to pamper yourself at least once or twice a month. Give yourself a little extra tender loving care. By giving yourself the gift of pampering, you will then be recharged, revitalized, and ready to give more to the world!

Giving, whether doing it or receiving it, is an elixir that builds up, encourages, and shows love. "Freely give," and see how you "freely receive" all of the wonderful benefits that will be "added to" your body, mind, and spirit.

Finally, think about the generous gift of salvation that God Himself gave to you. Truly, giving is a God principle. Make giving one of the principal things you do in life!

By giving to others, you give to *you*.

Giving:

- ▶ Releases the body's natural pain killers
- ▶ Strengthens your immune system
- ▶ Decreases the intensity and the awareness of physical pain
- ▶ Activates the emotions that are vital to the maintaining of good health
- ▶ Has multiple benefits to the body's system provided by stress relief

life-extender tip

"Freely you have received, freely give" (Matt. 10:8, NKJV). *It is better to give than to receive. Today give to someone who is in need.*

89

How can I rekindle a broken friendship?

Do you have any "fires" in your life today? If so, take the necessary steps to quench them while they are small with forgiveness, love, and compassion. Are you at odds with someone? The Bible advises us, "Do not let the sun go down on your anger" (Eph. 4:26, NAS). The longer you allow a grievance to fester, the bigger the internal fire becomes. This has serious ramifications on your spiritual fitness and your physical health. Discord brings disease to your body, mind, and spirit.

answer

Abraham Lincoln once said, "The better part of one's life consists of his friendships."[95] An entire new wave of studies shows the power of social connections. Positive relationships are crucial for your mental and physical health, while the absence of these life-enhancing relationships is very detrimental. Researchers are learning that the ties that bind are also the bonds that heal.[96]

The need for acceptance is built in, down to the very marrow of our bones. It is not a luxury; it is a necessity! It is imperative for you to douse any fires while they are small when it comes to being at odds with the people in your life whom you cherish. Otherwise, a small fire will soon become a wild fire, targeting your body, mind, and spirit! It has been said that people who have a lot of positive human contact can live twice as long as those who are isolated. It seems that the fewer number of human connections you have at home, at work, and in the community, the more likely you are to get sick, flood your brain with anxiety-causing chemicals, and die prematurely.

A friendship is a heart connection that literally makes your heart sing, your emotional health soar, and your physical health strong. It is imperative that you take steps to extinguish any "fires" of hurt and unforgiveness in your life right away so you will not fall victim to a wild fire, leaving you sick, discouraged, and floundering in the "ashes" of spiritual depletion. Remember that God calls you to be forgiving of others. When you forgive someone who may have wronged you, you are in an advantageous position to receive forgiveness from God.

When you lose the friendship of someone you deeply care about, it tends to call you back to your sense of values about what is truly important in life. The intangibles of love, hope, friendship, family togetherness, health, and peace of heart are far more valuable than any disagreement you may have had that has got you trapped in the "burning building" of despair!

Put out that fire with:

▶ Love
▶ Compassion
▶ Forgiveness

life-extender tip
Do you have any fires in your life? Put them out while they are small!

question

90

Should I step back and let my son and his wife make mistakes?

Are you concerned today about situations in someone else's life that seem to be out of their control? Do you feel pressured to keep on trying to "fix" a situation that seems impossible for you to fix? Are you growing weary and frustrated about it? It is in these situations you must remember that whatever is to be done or needs to be done in the situation, God is already doing. Now, take a deep breath and relax in this truth. Time itself will prove that God is and was always at work in every situation.

answer

Your earthly wisdom is limited. It tells you, "This is the way men and women have acted, responded, and lived through the ages." Your earthly wisdom concludes, "This is what works." Your advice to others can be very narrow-minded and filled with prejudices and personal agendas.

God's wisdom, in contrast, is unlimited. It is based upon what God sees when He looks back to ages past and ahead to ages still to come.

When it comes to you trying to "fix" others' problems, you must first ask yourself, "What does God want me to do? When? How? With whom? For what goal or purpose?"

We may live in the information age, but for all of our information, have we increased in wisdom? Our knowledge is limited. Not one of us can know exactly what to do in all situations or know all there is to know about any subject, person, or situation.

Before you step into a situation and try to fix it, you must step back and allow those you are concerned about to receive God's clear direction for their lives. This way, they will be spared many mistakes and false starts that may be the result of them listening only to your "earthly wisdom." Knowledge of the wisdom of God will keep your loved ones from making wrong decisions or entering into hurtful relationships. They will take fewer detours in life and experience fewer obstacles in their path!

When it comes to helping a loved one through a crisis, there is no one better qualified than God to guide their steps or to lead them into the right paths.

Share this wisdom from Proverbs 3:5–6 with your loved ones when they are going through a challenge: "Trust in the LORD with all your heart, and lean not on your own understanding; in all your ways acknowledge Him, and He shall direct your paths" (NKJV).

When considering how to help others, remember:

- ▶ Your earthly knowledge is limited.
- ▶ God's wisdom is unlimited.
- ▶ Others need a chance to grow in their faith with God by seeking His wisdom for themselves.
- ▶ God will come to their rescue as He is most qualified to guide their steps.

life-extender tip

Keep in mind that whatever is to be done, the Lord is doing!

91 What can I do to increase blessings in my life?

Often, we spend entirely too much time thinking about what we don't have, trials we are undergoing, and things we haven't accomplished. I challenge you instead to take time this day to count your blessings and be truly grateful for each one of them. You will find that this will lift your spirit, calm your mind, and fill your heart with joy. Giving thanks for blessings increases blessings. Adopt an attitude of gratitude today. As blessings increase, problems decrease.

answer

It seems that people who have the lives they want are people who have realized, on some level, that they deserve to have it. They truly believe that at any given moment, God is ready to give us new life, create new opportunities, miraculously heal situations, and change all darkness into light and all fear to love. God's light always shines bright, but it can sometimes appear tarnished by our illusions.

Blessings come when you take a breath and slow down. They come when you surrender all of your past hurts and future fears. They come when you truly have faith that God is at work on your behalf daily, forgiving, loving, strengthening, and healing you.

The first step on the road to increased blessings is to look back over your life, not with a critical eye, but rather to discover the connecting thread that gives your life rhythm and meaning. By recalling your life, you recollect yourself.

You gather together your forgotten priorities, passions, and blessings!

All too often, we focus on what we don't have, what we can't afford, what's missing from our lives. We want more and don't genuinely appreciate what we already have. When you shift your perspective, you will realize how much you have to be grateful for!

As you recognize the blessings in your life, stop a moment and give thanks. Give thanks for life itself. Give thanks for all of your resources—your ability to see, hear, taste, touch, speak, feel, think, love, and laugh. There is so much to be thankful for! Focus each day on what God has blessed you with—on what you have, whom you have, and what's right with your life. Adopt an attitude of gratitude, and watch the blessings flow!

Turn on your blessings by being continually aware of all of the blessings in your life:

▶ Are your basic needs taken care of?

▶ Do you have shelter, food, and clothing?

▶ Do you have friends and family that you can count on?

▶ Can you watch a sunset and listen to your favorite music?

▶ Can you smell the fragrance of your favorite flowers?

▶ Can you feel the warmth of the sun on your face?

▶ If so, my friend, you are blessed!

life-extender tip

Giving thanks for blessings increases blessings!

92   What can I do to be satisfied with the career I have?

Simone Weil once said, "If we go down into ourselves, we find that we possess exactly what we desire." Do you often spend time wishing that you were a better financial planner, carpenter, athlete, cook, singer, etc.? We all have abilities that are uniquely ours. We all have abilities that set us apart from the crowd. It is time for you to honor who you are and what abilities you have. They are gifts from God. If you honor them and find work putting these abilities to use, your work will become a source of joy and accomplishment. A job done well is a source of great satisfaction. So do it gladly!

answer

There is an old saying that says, "Bloom where you are planted," but I say, "Bloom where God has planted you!" God has equipped you with gifts that are uniquely yours. The problem is that we often look at others and their achievements, feeling inadequate when we do not accomplish the same. Instead, you should celebrate the talents of others while celebrating the gifts that God gave you.

When you realize that you do not have to accomplish what your best friend, family member, or co-worker has, then you can relax and let your God-given abilities shine forth. When you are operating out of your gifting, you will accomplish more!

When you honor the abilities you have, others will do the same. Doors will open to wonderful opportunities that would never have opened to you before because you were not operating with the knowledge that your gifting was uniquely yours. In other words, you become a "specialist." No one else can do your gifting as well as you! Once you realize this fact, your job satisfaction will increase tenfold!

If you are currently in a job that you feel is a wrong match for your God-given talent, begin to look for a new job that closely mirrors your gifts. In the meantime, bloom where you are planted. Doing your best work will bring you joy and satisfaction while you wait with great expectation for the new vocation that will match your gifts!

Magnify your God-given ability by:

▶ Honoring your gift
▶ Putting your gifts to use
▶ Doing your job well

life-extender tip

God has given each of us the ability to do certain things well. (See Romans 12:6.) So do them gladly.

93 I am tired of trying to solve my problems alone. Can you help?

Are you feeling overwhelmed with the pressure of trying to solve your problems? It's true that life can be challenging for even the most "together" person you know. When you have stretched your own problem-solving resources to the max and still come up short, there is help.

answer

Today why not ask God for what you need instead of trying to do it all yourself? God made us to seek fellowship with Him. There are times when we need His help and simply need to go to Him in prayer and ask. It is in prayer that we can expose our true selves and deepest needs. We can be who we really are, transparent, shields down, underbellies exposed. God knows us. He knows our hearts. He knows what we need before we even ask. He is just waiting. Ask Him today!

God created us to be His friends, but over time, our lives have gotten so busy or too complicated that we often leave little time for Him. Those are the very times we try to go it alone, without the comfort, wisdom, and energy His friendship offers.

What's more is that people with faith-filled allegiance are less likely to experience physical illness, mental symptoms, or difficulties keeping strong relationships. Asking for God's help and trusting in His divine power are truly the pathway to optimal mental and physical health. Opening your heart to God will enrich your life in ways you never thought possible.

Studies are beginning to show the connection between faith and recovery. Those who attended religious services more than once a week enjoyed seven years longer life expectancy than those who never attended. Older adults who considered themselves religious functioned better and had fewer problems than those without faith. Adults who attend a house of worship have lower rates of depression and anxiety.[97]

As you can see, the evidence supports the notion that trust in someone outside of yourself actually releases healing hormones into your body that contribute to the healing process. Those who, beneath all the concerns and worries that face them, have an underlying trust that says all things will ultimately work out for good are able to gather resources that contribute to their healing in ways that others are not able to do.[98]

When faced with problems and there seems to be nowhere to turn, just ask! William Inge once said, "Faith begins as an experiment and ends in an experience!"[99]

How to become acquainted with your "divine friend":

▶ Pray: Prayer is open, fearless, honest talk with God, anytime and any place.

▶ Study Scripture: This is God's letter to you!

▶ Find your quiet place: Find your favorite "meeting place" for you and God to commune.

▶ People: Follow the lead of people who know God's power. Ask questions. They know the path!

life-extender tip

Ask for help from God, and you will receive it.
(See Psalm 46:1; Matthew 7:7.)

question

94

How can I develop a closer relationship with God?

Many people have a hard time understanding how to develop a close relationship with God, who seems so far away. How can He be reached if He can't be seen? How can He comfort if He can't be touched? God has made a way for you to know Him, access His divine resources, and feel His loving presence.

answer

Developing a close relationship with God begins with prayer. If prayer is not a part of your daily life, I encourage you to begin today. Prayer changes lives—not just yours, but also the lives of those you love. There are three practical steps to help you develop an attitude of trust in God.

1. *Communicate.* Trust grows in an atmosphere of honesty and openness. God has been honest with you. It is time to be honest with Him as well. In prayer, you can do just that. Prayer is nothing more than talking to God and listening with your heart for answers.

2. *Listen.* Be open to what God reveals about Himself in the Bible. In order to trust someone, you have to get to know them, right? To really get a close-up of God's character, read the Gospels of Matthew, Mark, Luke, and John, which are accounts of Christ's life on Earth. They will provide you with a close-up picture of God and His true nature.

3. *Ask.* Ask for God's help in specific areas in your life. And keep on asking! You will begin to learn more and more from the way He answers. Realize that a no can be just as instructive as His yes to your prayers. Asking

will "exercise" your faith. Faith moves mountains! It has been said that courage is simply fear that has said its prayers.

As you implement a life of prayer, fears leave and courage takes up residence! "You will keep in perfect peace all who trust in you, whose thoughts are fixed on you!" (Isa. 26:3, NLT).

Your days can be filled with an overflowing joy if you begin your day by spending time with God, reading His Word, praying, and listening for direction. When you pray, you need to stop and listen. Sometimes you may hear God as a still, small voice from deep within your heart, and suddenly, you know what you should or should not do. God is listening for your prayers. He also likes it when you listen to His answers too!

Through prayer, you can be rooted, established, strong, immovable, and determined, knowing that whatever you may face today, He will complete you and make you what He created you to be. He will establish you and ground you securely, strengthen and settle you. It is with prayer that His assurance is your "insurance"!

Develop a closer relationship with God by:

- ▶ Keeping in touch with God and staying tuned to His voice
- ▶ Getting in the "flow" of God's river of life and learn to "float" in the power of His presence
- ▶ Praising Him daily
- ▶ Keeping your hands open and ready to receive from Him
- ▶ Serving Him
- ▶ Reading and studying His Word

life-extender tip

Develop a closer relationship with God through prayer. Communicate, listen, and ask!

Are you experiencing a dark time in your life right now? Have you or are you experiencing a loss, death of a loved one, a bitter divorce, unemployment, or illness? All of us will experience loss before our time on Earth here is done. We live day to day, not knowing from moment to moment what we will have to face. We live not knowing what tomorrow holds. Take comfort that your tomorrow is not in the hands of your boss, your spouse, your children, your friends, or your family. No one can manipulate or dominate your tomorrow. Your tomorrow is in the hands of God. He is there when money, husbands, wives, friends, jobs, and children are gone.

answer

If you are going through a "wilderness experience," remember your life has a purpose. Sometimes it is far beyond your comfort, ease, or pleasure. Your life is intended to be used by God to fulfill His purposes on earth.

Yes, you may be going through a dark night of the soul, but just as night passes and morning breaks, this dark time shall pass, and joy will come in the morning. In my life, I have always found that God has always brought joy to me right after the "mourning."

With this in mind, you can take courage that no matter what you may be facing, God will give you courage, strength, and comfort when you ask Him for it. Your end point is often God's starting point!

God has a plan and purpose for your life as a whole. With each experience, He is continually in the process of preparing you to be a person with whom He intends to live forever!

In every experience you must trust that God has a perfecting good as the final outcome.

There is an eternal purpose for all that happens: "'For my thoughts are not your thoughts, nor are your ways My ways,' says the LORD. 'For as the heavens are higher than earth, so are My ways higher than your ways, and My thoughts than your thoughts'" (Isa. 55:8–9, NKJV).

With this in mind, count it all joy!

The wilderness has a blessing on the other side that will:

▶ Lead you to a more spiritual place in life
▶ Heal you in places you need to grow
▶ Grow you in ways you need to grow

life-extender tip

Realize that whatever you are facing, joy comes in the morning! "Weeping may endure for a night, but joy comes in the morning" (Ps. 30:5, NKJV).

question

96 How can I make the pressures of life stop without disappointing anyone?

There comes a time in everyone's life when the demands are too great. Sometimes these demands may be pressure from work, family members, or friends. While all of these things are important to you, it is equally important that you stop doing things for them that you really do not have the energy or time to do. If not, you essentially give your "power" away. You are being drained!

answer

A good tip-off that you are being drained is putting up with things that you would rather not. There is a cost to saying yes to energy drains that can literally "suck the life out of you."

"Energy vampires," as I call them, cost you. It may be your money, your time, and possibly your health due to the added stress. Creating loving boundaries is about honoring your integrity, your needs, and your desire to create a happier, healthier, and more balanced life!

Saying no to things becomes easy when you learn to express yourself from your heart and speak through your values. In other words, if you stay true to who you are, your words will follow.

Create loving boundaries by:

▶ *Regarding your values*: Your values are the beliefs you have that allow you to make choices from your heart, and they enable you to engage in actions that bring joy and energy into your life. Without boundaries, you limit your beliefs. This will keep you from experiencing your deeper values, which results in keeping you from moving forward with your own desires.

▶ *Having inner strength*: Your inner strength is your ability to listen to your heart and make balanced, healthy choices for your life.

▶ *Maintaining balance*: Balance is your ability to look at circumstances, through the foundation of your values, and to choose the actions that do not drain your energy.

▶ *Standing your ground*: Standing your ground comes from a place of "inner strength." There is energy in being who you really are. You are saying no to satisfy your true feelings and saying yes to your boundaries.

▶ *Building trust*: Trust that by creating boundaries, you can live with more integrity and communicate more authentically—and that will honor all involved!

Finally, you cannot be all things to all people. But there is One who can. If you feel yourself being drained, just plug into your "supreme energy force"—God!

Not setting good boundaries costs you:

▶ Money
▶ Time
▶ Good health

life-extender tip

Create boundaries in your life. Say enough! Direct those you love to God, who is their endless source, rather than you being that endless source!

97 How can I heal from a long-standing condition?

I encourage you to "get real" in all areas of your life. It is time to unearth and discard things that are weighing you down. You must deal with the past and all of its issues. Your true nature is not one of pain, sickness, and mental anguish. God did not design you that way. You must get real with who you really are. By dealing with issues that have held you back from being all of what God intended you to be, you will be well on your way to living life whole, healed, and free!

answer

When dealing with chronic illness, many times negative emotions such as anger, unforgiveness, fear, or guilt may be one of the causative factors. These dangerous emotions can create a pathway to illness.

You must release all negative emotions—resentment, envy, fear, sadness, and anger. Express your feelings; don't hold on to them. You must start to do things that bring you a sense of fulfillment, joy, and purpose and that validate your worth.

Pay close attention to yourself by nourishing and encouraging yourself. Love yourself and everyone else. Make loving a primary expression in your life. Keep your sense of humor. Accept yourself and everything in your life as an opportunity for growth and learning. Make some sort of positive contribution to your community through some sort of work or service that you enjoy. Try to heal any wounds from past relationships.

Many times, when you are suffering from chronic illness, spiritual depletion takes place due to anxiety, depression, and the stress that come from having the physical condition. One of the greatest healing miracles of all time is—spirituality. Having faith can speed recovery from physical and mental illness, surgery, and addiction. Pray, be grateful, and give thanks to God continually. Faith gives you a sense of peace and an ability to help you look beyond your present problems with hope. It reduces stress and therefore increases your chance of recovery.

The real you is healthy, vibrant, and strong. Get real and give your body, mind, and spirit the God-given potential to heal. You are worth it!

How do you become ill?

▶ Blame others for your problems
▶ Do not express your feelings and views openly and honestly
▶ Be resentful and hypercritical, especially toward yourself
▶ Keep pushing yourself, no matter how overstressed and tired you are
▶ Avoid deep, long-lasting relationships
▶ Worry most, if not all, of the time
▶ Follow everyone else's advice while seeing yourself as miserable and stuck
▶ Don't have a sense of humor; life is no laughing matter
▶ Be a victim of self-pity, envy, and anger

life-extender tip

In order to heal, you must deal and get real!

98

How do I overcome the fear of moving forward?

Isaiah 41:10 says, "Do not fear, for I [God] am with you" (NIV). Fear is a killer of dreams, hopes, relationships, and careers. Many times, fear has limited your potential, excluded possibilities, and controlled your choices. Fear may have played a part in your likes and dislikes, picked your friends, and even raised your children and walked down the aisle with you as you married. Fear stands between you and your ability to go anywhere you like, do anything you want, and meet anyone you please. To help keep you safe, fear motivates you to hide your true nature by limiting your ability to express yourself truthfully. Faith, on the other hand, casts out fear!

answer

Winston Churchill summed it up brilliantly years ago when he stated, "The only thing we have to fear is fear itself." The Bible also gives us words of God that I call "fear busters."

> Even though I walk through the valley of the shadow of death, I will fear no evil, for you are with me: your rod and your staff, they comfort me.
>
> —Psalm 23:4, NIV

> For God hath not given us the spirit of fear; but of power, and of love, and of a sound mind.
>
> —2 Timothy 1:7, KJV

> There is no fear in love; but perfect love casts out
> fear, because fear involves torment. But he who
> fears has not been made perfect in love.
>
> —1 John 4:18, NKJV

> The LORD is my light and my salvation—whom
> shall I fear? The LORD is the stronghold of my
> life—of whom shall I be afraid?
>
> —Psalm 27:1, NIV

Fear is both the cause and effect of the feelings, thoughts, or actions that prohibit you from accepting yourself and realizing your full potential. Fear is the gatekeeper of your comfort zone. But many people who live in fear use their comfort zone as a bunker to shield them from living life fearlessly. When you become fearless, fear turns into your guidance system. Fear then can propel you forward again and again as you confidently take the very risks that keep you free from fear itself!

As a child of God, you can tap into the truth of who you really are. You can then awake to the wonder of living fearlessly, without any more excuses or regrets, all the days of your life!

Living without fear is about:

▶ Enjoying the thrill of a challenging situation instead of shrinking from it

▶ Exploring with curiosity and creativity without fear of being ridiculed

▶ Living each moment instead of wasting time getting ready to live

life-extender tip

Examine your life to see if fear is in any way controlling you. The opposite of faith is fear!

99

What is spiritual depletion?

If you find yourself suffering from anxiety, depression, stress, and resultant physical illness, spiritual depletion has most likely taken place. If you neglect your spiritual health, you cannot experience total wellness and longevity. All of us have a "God-shaped" hole in our hearts that only He can fill. Deep within us, there is a longing to be fed from the hand of God.

answer

Food for your soul is just as important as nourishment to your body. When human arms fail to hold you, there is always the strength of the everlasting arms of God. If you are suffering from anxiety, depression, or unrelenting stress, I suggest that you develop a closer relationship first with God and secondly with yourself. By doing so, you will develop spiritually and strengthen yourself and your personality. When each area is strengthened, you will be able to clearly discern where you need to bring the changes that put balance back into your life.

Spiritual depletion goes hand in hand with anxiety, depression, and stress. It is a sure sign that your life has become unmanageable and that you have lost your way. Balance cannot be attained apart from God. It cannot be done without prayer. It's as if He knew that if we could successfully balance life without Him, we would become so self-reliant that we would forget the One who gave our lives to us in the first place.

When your life falls apart, He is the One who holds it together. Often when pain comes into your life, a birth is imminent. So think of your trials as birthing pains that will deliver the true destiny God is birthing in your life. Think of your trial as a sure sign that God is ready to deliver!

I am here to tell you that there is a way to find your "true north" again. It is a journey, taken step by step, one day at a time.

Finally, the Lord is your comforter in the midst of all of your trials and situations that make you anxious, stressed, or depressed. In the midst of situations that seem to have no rhyme or reason, beyond all of the madness, there is a God. He catches your tears and collects your pain.

He holds your tomorrow. His grace will bring you through!

The way home:

- ▶ Pray: Pray for strength because He gives might when you have none.
- ▶ Praise: Praise God for your survival because you know it is by His mercy that you are still here.
- ▶ Pamper: It is through pampering yourself that you find renewal and comfort against the tragedies of life![100]

life-extender tip

Read God's Word. It is food to the body.
Feed your soul today!

100

What are the basics to keeping myself alive and happy for the long haul?

I cannot stress the importance of investing in all three areas of your earthly experience—the body as we discussed in part one, the mind in part two, and your spirit in part three. The choice is yours. By reading this book, you have taken the first step. Now, you must implement what you have learned. Making healthy choices a part of your life is the key to extending your days, making the rest of your life the best of your life—from health to eternity!

answer

Here are some life-extending highlights:

▶ Good nutrition is the fuel that drives your entire system. Take what you have learned and evaluate your food intake, remembering that even small improvements done on a regular basis multiply health benefits and therefore extend your days.

▶ Your faith, beliefs, and hopes all affect your health. Trust in God underlines the importance of faith's relationship between spirituality and healing.

▶ Your outlook colors your perspective on life. Your outlook's influence on your mind can affect your body and, therefore, impact the progression or healing from disease.

▶ Friends are flowers in the garden of life. Watering your friendships and knowing that you have the support of others will contribute to improved health and life extension.

▶ An increase in activity translates directly into improved health and longevity. Activity includes walking, stretching, weight training, and aerobic activity.

▶ Rest, repair, rejuvenate, and regenerate with a good night's sleep and taking time out for relaxation during the day. Take a weekend vacation. Take "mini vacations" in your mind each day.

▶ Take steps to make your environment a healthy place. Your environment is what lies outside your body but has an impact on what takes place within you.

Do you want a longer life? Would you like to know how to recover from illness? Do you wish all of your relationships were strong and filled with peace? Do you want more joy and peace of mind each day? Do you want more energy for your day? If so, why not invest? You are worth it!

As I wrote this book, my hope was to inspire you to do all of the things needed to enjoy life. My goal was to show you that there is a better way to live this one life that you have been given. My commitment was to show you that you can get there!

Now I challenge you to:

▶ Take what you have learned and share it with all the people you love and want to spend long days with, happily, peacefully, and glowing with health

▶ Make a commitment to live a balanced life

▶ Turn to God for strength, encouragement, and help

life-extender tip

Recommit to invest yourself completely—body, mind, and spirit.

Conclusion

The late George Burns summed it up brilliantly when he said, "If I knew that I was going to live this long, I would have taken better care of myself." I have given you one hundred ways to do just that. All of these antiaging tips are based upon one hundred of the most commonly asked questions concerning longevity.

Typically, many of us start to slowly go "downhill" in our early forties. As we move into our midfifties, we get a little fatter, weaker, slower, and less sure-footed as more medical and orthopedic problems surface. Arthritis, high blood pressure, type 2 diabetes, and elevated cholesterol become the traveling companions of midlife.

By the time we move into our midsixties, many of us will be on five or six different medications. Our hair turns gray or disappears. Our skin loses its elasticity, and our muscle mass decreases. We sit more and move less. Some even give up on life as they lose their independence.

The good news is that *now* we know that for most of us these illnesses are the result of lifestyle problems that go back over thirty years. In other words, our lifestyles in our younger days often contribute to disease in our forties, fifties, sixties, and beyond. A large percentage of heart attacks, common cancers, strokes, diabetes, falls, fractures, serious injuries, and illnesses are from choices we have made. Getting older is inevitable; feeling older is optional.

By becoming proactive in terms of your health by incorporating these one hundred antiaging tips, you do not have to follow down the same path that your parents and grandparents traveled. Knowledge has increased concerning the prevention of most degenerative diseases associated with the aging process. This explosion of knowledge is yours for the taking. We are a generation blessed with the tools and modalities to not only extend life but also enhance the quality of our years.

As I conclude this body of work, I will leave you with seven antiaging super prescriptions. I wish you long life, complete with vibrant health to enjoy many sunsets, much love, and the joy of watching your children, grandchildren, and great-grandchildren flourish!

Yours in vibrant health,

Dr. Janet

	Organic Green Tea
Antiaging Super Prescription **#1**	Green tea contains a rich source of antioxidants and substances that assist detoxification. Drink organic green tea regularly (two cups or more daily), or take 500 to 1,500 mg of the capsule form.
	Green Superfood Supplement
Antiaging Super Prescription **#2**	Take an organic green superfood such as chlorella or spirulina, or a mixture of these each day. Take as directed on the bottle. You may take capsules, powder, or liquid form.
	Essential Fatty Acids
Antiaging Super Prescription **#3**	Daily take 1 to 2 tablespoons of flaxseed oil, 3 grams of fish oil, or a formulation that contains a mixture of omega-3, -6, and -9 fatty acids.
	High-Potency Multivitamin
Antiaging Super Prescription **#4**	Take a high-potency multivitamin and mineral formula daily; it contains a strong base of the antioxidants and other nutrients that protect against aging.

	Garlic (allium sativum)
Antiaging Super Prescription **#5**	Take one to two capsules of an aged garlic product daily. Garlic benefits the immune and cardiovascular systems. It also improves detoxification and has antioxidant properties. You may also take garlic in the form of a liquid extract.
	Gingko Biloba
Antiaging Super Prescription **#6**	Take 60 to 120 mg twice daily of a standardized product containing 24 percent flavone glycosides and 6 percent terpene lactones. Gingko improves circulation, has potent antioxidant properties, improves memory, and reduces one's tendency to get blood clots. Avoid if you are taking blood-thinning medication.
	Siberian Ginseng (*Eleutherococcus senticosus*)
Antiaging Super Prescription **#7**	Take 600 to 900 mg of a standardized product daily. As with most types of ginseng, *eleutherococcus* works to help the body adapt to mental and physical stress.[101]

Notes

1. This answer is taken from: Shreelata Suresh, "Eating for Balance," About.com: Holistic Healing, http://healing .about.com/od/ayurvedic_diet/ss/eatforbalance.htm (accessed March 9, 2009); "Ayurvedic Medicine: An Introduction," National Center of Complementary and Alternative Medicine, http://nccam.nih.gov/health/ ayurveda/introduction.htm (accessed March 9, 2009).

2. Boomers TV, "10 Ways to Lower Your RealAge," Boomers! RedefiningLifeAfterFifty, http://www.boomerstv.com/tips_ sample.php?group_id=19 (accessed April 13, 2009).

3. G. M. Cole and S. A. Frautschy, "Docosahexaenoic Acid Protects From Amyloid and Dendritic Pathology in an Alzheimer's Disease Mouse Mode," *Nutrition Health* 18, no. 3 (2006): 249–259; P. Barberger-Gateau, C. Raffaitin, and L. Letenneur, "Dietary Patterns and Risk of Dementia: The Three-City Cohort Study," *Neurology* 69 (2007): 1921–1930.

4. Penny M. Kris-Etherton, William S. Harris, and Lawrence J. Appel, "Fish Consumption, Fish Oil, Omega-3 Fatty Acids, and Cardiovascular Diseases," *Circulation* 106, no. 21 (November 19, 2002): 2747–2757; Erratum in *Circulation* 107, no. 3 (January 28, 2003): 512.

5. J. Guz, T. Dziaman, and A. Szpila, "Do Antioxidant Vitamins Influence Carcinogenesis?" *Postepy Higieny Medycyny Doswiadczalnej* (Warszawa) 61 (2007): 1851–1898.

6. DicQie Fuller, PhD, DSc, *The Healing Power of Enzymes* (n.p.: Forbes, Inc., 1998).

7. *Molecular and Cellular Biochemistry* 246, nos. 1–2 (April 2003): 75–82.

8. Y. Hanaki, S. Sugiyama, and T. Ozwawa, "Ratio of Low Density Lipoprotein Cholesterol to Ubiquinone as a Coronary Risk Factor," *New England Journal of Medicine* 325, no. 11 (September 1991): 814–815.

9. R. McCaleb, "Anticancer Effects of Garlic—More Proof," *HerbalGram* 27 (1992): 22–23.

10. S. Foster, "Garlic," Botanical Series 311 (Austin, TX: American Botanical Council, 1991).

11. F. Bertolini, L. Fusetti, C. Rabascio, S. Cinieri, G. Martinelli, and G. Pruneri, "Inhibition of Angiogenesis and Induction of Endothelial and Tumor Cell Apoptosis by Green Tea in Animal Models of Human High-Grade non-Hodgkin's Lymphoma," *Leukemia* 14, no. 8 (August 2000): 1477–1482.

12. Y. Kuwahara, S. Kono, H. Eguchi, H. Hamada, K. Shinchi, and K. Imanishi, "Relationship Between Serologically Diagnosed Chronic Atrophic Gastritis, Helicobacter Pylori, and Environmental Factors in Japanese Men," *Scandinavian Journal of Gastroenterology* 35 no. 5 (May 2000): 476–481.

13. Hasan Mukhtar and Nihal Ahmad, "Tea Polyphenols: Prevention of Cancer and Optimizing Health," *American Journal of Clinical Nutrition* 71, no. 6 (June 2000): 1698S–1702S.

14. C. J. Dufresne and E. R. Farnworth, "A Review of Latest Research Findings on the Health Promotion Properties of Tea," *Journal of Nutritional Biochemistry* 12, no. 7 (2001): 404–421; C. L. Sun, J. M. Yuan, M. J. Lee, et al., "Urinary Tea Polyphenols in Relation to Gastric and Esophageal Cancers: A Prospective Study of Men in Shanghai, China," *Carcinogenesis* 23, no. 9 (2002): 1497–1503.

15. G. E. Fraser, J. Sabeté, W. L. Beeson, et al. "A Possible Protective Effect of Nut Consumption on Risk of Coronary Heart Disease (The Adventist Health Study)," *Archives of Internal Medicine* 152 (1992): 1416–1424.

16. G. E. Fraser, D. Sumbureru, P. Pribis, et al., "Association Among Health Habits, Risk Factors, and All Cause Mortality in a Black California Population," *Epidemiology* 8 (1997): 168–174.

17. F. B. Hu and M. J. Stamfer, "Nut Consumption and Risk of Coronary Heart Disease: A Review of the Epidemiologic Evidence," *Current Atherosclerosis Reports* 1 (1999): 204–209; G. E. Fraser and D. J. Shavik, "Ten Years of Life: Is It a Matter of Choice?" *Archives of Internal Medicine* 161 (2001): 1645–1652.

18. Selene Yeager and the editors of *Prevention* magazine, "Mushrooms: The Healing Fungus," in *The Doctors Book of Food Remedies*, (New York: Rodale Press, 2007), 439.

19. This answer is taken from: W. Stahl and H. Sies, "Lycopene: A Biologically Important Carotenoid for Humans," *Archives of Biochemistry and Biophysics* 336 (1996): 1–9; H. Gerster, "The Potential Role of Lycopene for Human Health," *Journal of the American College of Nutrition* 16 (1997): 109–126; Harvard Health Publications, "Tomatoes and Prostate Cancer," March 5, 2002, https://www.health.harvard.edu/newsweek/ Tomatoes_Prostate_Cancer.htm (accessed June 1, 2009).

20. John F. Kennedy, speech given at Newport at the dinner before the America's Cup Races, September 1962, as quoted by The Quotations Page, Quotation # 36911 of Classic Quotes, http://www.quotationspage.com/ quote/36911.html (accessed January 28, 2009).

21. Barbara Hendel and Peter Ferreira, *Water and Salt: The Essence of Life* (n.p.: Natural Resources, Inc., 2003).

22. This answer is taken from: W. C. Willett, "Diet and Coronary Heart Disease," *Monographs in Epidemiology* 379 (1990); World Health Organization, "Diet, Nutrition, and the Prevention of Chronic Disease in a Study Group, *WHO Technical Report Series* (Geneva) 797 (1990); E. Gimeno, M. Fitó, R. M. Lamuela-Raventós, et al., Effect of Ingestion of Virgin Olive Oil on Human Low-density Lipoprotein Composition, *European Journal of Clinical Nutrition* 56, no. 2 (February 2002): 114–120.

23. This answer is taken from: Adriane Fugh Berman, MD, *Alternative Medicine: What Works*, (n.p.: Lippencott, Williams, and Wilkins, 1997).

24. Colette Bouchez, "Make the Most of Your Metabolism," WebMD.com, http://www.webmd.com/fitness-exercise/ guide/make-most-your-metabolism (accessed January 29, 2009).

25. R. Bella, R. Biondi, R. Raffaele, et al., "Effect of Acetyl L Carnitine on Geriatric Patients Suffering From Dysthymic Disorders," *International Journal of Clinical Pharmacology Research* 10 (1990): 355–360.

26. Yeager and the editors of *Prevention* magazine, *The Doctors Book of Food Remedies*, 222.

27. "Eat Smart," *USA Weekend*, January 12, 1997, http://www.usaweekend.com/food/carper_archive/ 970112carper_eatsmart.html (accessed April 13, 2009).

28. Ibid.

29. Rita Elkins, *Bee Pollen, Royal Jelly, Propolis and Honey* (n.p.: Woodland Publishing, 1996).

30. This answer is taken from: K. C. Kim and I. G. Kim, "Ganoderma Lucidum Extracts Protects DNA From Strand Breakage Caused by Hydroxylradical and UV Irradiation," *International Journal of Molecular Medicine* 4, no. 3 (September 1999): 273–277.

31. "The History of Herbal Medicine," Your Family Doctor: Online-Ambulance.com, http://www.online-ambulance.com/altermed/grp/Herbal_Medicine/pg/1/art/herbal_medicine_chest.html (accessed March 9, 2009); J. Kleijen and P. Knipschild, "Gingko Biloba," *Lancet* 340, no.8828 (November 1992): 1136–1139.

32. P. Braquest, ed., "Ginkolides—Chemistry, Biology, Pharmacology and Clinical Perspectives," *Prous Science* 2 (1998).

33. P. L. Le Bars, M. M. Katz, N. Berman, T. M. Itil, A. M. Freedman, and A. F. Schatzberg, "A Placebo-Controlled, Double-Blind Randomized Trial of an Extract of Gingko Biloba for Dementia" (North American EGb Study Group), *Journal of the American Medical Association* 278, no. 16 (October 22, 1997): 1327–1332.

34. "Chlordane Found in Foods Decades After Pesticide Use," Press Release of the American Chemical Society, May 2, 2000, as quoted on ScienceBlog.com, http://www.scienceblog.com/community/older/2000/A/200000253.html (accessed March 9, 2009).

35. "Toxicology Profile for Chlordane," Agency for Toxic Substances and Disease Registry, http://www.atsdr.cdc.gov/toxprofiles/tp31.html (accessed March 9, 2009).

36. The Editors of Sportline, *The Benefits of Walking: Sportline's Guide to Walking* (n.p.: E & B Giftware, 2004), 2.

37. Oscar H. Franko, Chris de Laet, Anna Peters, Jacqueline Jonker, Johan Mackenbach, and Wilma Nusselder, "Effects of Physical Activity on Life Expectancy With Cardiovascular Disease," *Archives of Internal Medicine* 165, no 20 (November 14, 2005): 2355–2360.

38. Suvi Rovio, Ingemar Kareholt, and Eeva-Liisa Helkala, "Leisure-time Physical Activity at Midlife and the Risk of Dementia and Alzheimer's Disease," *The Lancet Neurology* 4, no. 11 (November 2005): 705–711, http://www.thelancet.com/journals/laneur/article/PIIS1474-4422(05)70198-8/fulltext (accessed April 13, 2009); Eric Larson, Li Wang, James D. Bowen, et al., "Exercise Is Associated With Reduced Risk for Incident Dementia Among Persons Sixty-Five Years of Age and Older," *Annals of Internal Medicine* 144, no. 2 (January 17, 2006): 73–81, http://www.annals.org/cgi/content/full/144/2/73#FN (accessed April 13, 2009).

39. William T. Greenough, Neal J. Cohen, and Janice M. Juraska, "New Neurons in Old Brains: Learning to Survive?" *Nature Neuroscience* 2 (1999), 203–205.

40. K. L. Tucker, K. Morita, N. Qiao, et al., "Colas, but Not Other Carbonated Beverages Are Associated With Low Bone Density in Older Women" (The Framingham Osteoporosis Study), *American Journal of Clinical Nutrition* 84, no. 4 (October 2006): 936–942.

41. Elson M. Haas, MD, "Phosphorus," http://www.healthy.net/scr/article.asp?ID=2061 (accessed March 9, 2009), excerpted from Elson M. Haas, MD, *Staying Healthy With Nutrition: The Complete Guide to Diet and Nutritional Medicine* (n.p.: Celestial Arts, 2006).

42. F. M. Gloth III, C. M. Gundberg, B. W. Hollis, J. G. Haddad Jr., and J. D. Tobin, "Vitamin D Deficiency in Homebound Elderly Persons," *Journal of the American Medical Association* 274, no. 21 (December 6, 1995): 1683–1686; *Bone* 30, no. 5 (May 2002): 771–777.

43. Michael F. Holick, "Sunlight and Vitamin D for Bone Health and Prevention of Autoimmune Diseases, Cancers, and Cardiovascular Disease," *American Journal of Clinical Nutrition* 80, no. 6 (December 2004): 1678S–1688S.

44. *British Journal of Dermatology* 122, no. 35 (April 1990): S13–S20.

45. Adrienne Dellwo, "HPA Axis," About.com, http://chronicfatigue.about.com/od/cfsglossary/g/hpa_axis.htm (accessed March 26, 2009).

46. J. Liu, S. Wang, H. Liu, et al., "Stimulatory Effect of Saponin From Panax Ginseng on Immune Function of Lymphocytes in the Elderly," *Mechanisms of Aging and Development* 83, no. 1 (1995): 43–53, as quoted in Melissa Schweikhart, "Ginseng," http://www.vanderbilt.edu/AnS/psychology/health_psychology/ginseng.htm (accessed March 9, 2009).

47. Y. S. Huo, "Anti Senility Action of Saponins in Panax Ginseng Fruit in 327 Cases," *Chung Hsi I Chieh Ho Tsa Chih* 4, no. 10 (October 1984): 578, 593–596; C. N. Joo, "The Preventative Effect of Korean (P. Ginseng) Saponins on Aortic Atheroma Formation in Prolonged Cholesterol-Fed Rabbits," Proceedings of the Third International Ginseng Synposium (1980): 27–36; F. Scoglione, F. Ferrara, S. Dugnani, et al., "Immunomodulatory Effects of Two Extracts of Panax Ginseng C.A. Meyer," *Drugs Under Experimental and Clinical Research* 16 (1990): 537–542.

48. FDA.gov, "Cyclamate Update," May 16, 1989, http://www.fda.gov/bbs/topics/ANSWERS/ANS00155.html (accessed March 9, 2009).

49. Mike Adams, "Artificial Sweeteners," NaturalPedia: NaturalNews.com, http://www.artificial-sweeteners.org/Artificial_sweetener-3.html (accessed January 30, 2009).

50. Yeager and the editors of *Prevention* magazine, *The Doctors Book of Food Remedies*, 39.

51. Janet Star Hull, "Food Additives to Avoid," http://www.sweetpoison.com/food-additives-to-avoid.html (accessed February 2, 2009).

52. Center for Science in the Public Interest, "Food Additives," http://www.cspinet.org/reports/chemcuisine.htm (accessed February 2, 2009).

53. Hull, "Food Additives to Avoid."

54. Ibid.

55. Ibid.

56. WebMD.com, "Baby Boomers Listen Up: Ear Today, Gone Tomorrow," WebMD Men's Health Feature, September 13, 2001, http://men.webmd.com/features/baby-boomers-listen-up (accessed February 2, 2009).

57. Daniel J. DeNoon, "Folic Acid May Slow Hearing Loss," WebMD Health News, January 2, 2007, http://www.webmd.com/news/20070102/folic-acid-may-slow-hearing-loss (accessed February 2, 2009).

58. Miranda Hitti, "Nutrient Combo May Curb Hearing Loss," WedMD Health News, March 30, 2007, http://www.webmd.com/food-recipes/news/20070330/nutrient-comb-may-curb-hearing-loss (accessed February 2, 2009).

59. J. Constant, "Alcohol, Ischemic Heart Disease, and the French Paradox," *Coronary Artery Disease* 8, no. 10 (October 1997): 645–649; J. D. Folts, "Potential Health Benefits From the Flavonoids in Grape Products on Vascular Disease," *Advances in Experimental Medicine and Biology* 505 (2002): 95–111; Luis Bujanda, Maria Garcia-Barcina, Virginia Gutierrez-de Juan, et al., "Effect of Resveratrol on Alcohol-Induced Mortality and Liver Lesions in Mice," *BMC Gastroenterology* 6 (November 14, 2006): 35, viewed at http://www.pubmedcentral.nih.gov/articlerender.fcgi?artid=1657014 (accessed March 9, 2009).

60. Linda Page, *Linda Page's Healthy Healing* (n.p.: Healthy Healing Inc., 2004), 464.

61. This answer is taken from: O. M. Wolkowitz, V. I. Reus, A. Keebler, et al., "Double-Blind Treatment of Major Depression With Dehydroepiandrosterone," *American Journal of Psychiatry* 156 (April 1999): 646–649, viewed at http://ajp.psychiatryonline.org/cgi/content/full/156/4/646 (accessed March 9, 2009); G. Patti, R. Melfi, and G. Di Sciascio, "The Role of Endothelial Dysfunction in the Pathogenesis and in Clinical Practice of Artherosclerosis: Current Evidences," *Recenti Progressi in Medicina* 96, no. 10 (October 2005): 499–507; H. Hougaku, J. L. Fleg, S. S. Najjar, et al, "Relationship Between Androgenic Hormones and Arterial Stiffness, Based on Longitudinal Hormone Measurements," *American Journal of Physiology—Endocrinology and Metabolism* 290, no. 2 (February 2006): E234–E242; F. Labtrie, P. Diamond, L. Cusan, et al., "Effect of Twelve-Month Dehydroepiandrosterone Replacement Therapy on Bone, Vagina, and Endometrium in Postmenopausal Women," *Journal of Clinical Endocrinology and Metabolism* 82, no. 10 (October 1997): 3498–3505, viewed at http://jcem.endojournals.org/cgi/content/full/82/10/3498 (accessed March 9, 2009).

62. E. Ostman, Y. Granfeldt, L. Persson, and I. Bjorck, "Vinegar Supplementation Lowers Glucose and Insulin Responses and Increase Satiety After a Bread Meal in Healthy Subjects," *European Journal of Clinical Nutrition* 59, no. 9 (September 2005): 983–988.

63. TheWBALChannel.com, "Berry Pack Cancer-Fighting Punch," July 1, 2006, as quoted at http://www .oralcancerfoundation.org/news/news.asp?offset=750 (accessed February 4, 2009).

64. M. I. Sweeney, W. Kalt, S. L. MacKinnon, et al., "Feeding Rats Diets Enriched in Lowbush Blueberries for Six Weeks Decreases Ischemia-Induced Brain Damage," *Nutritional Neuroscience* 5, no. 6 (December 2002): 427–431.

65. Yeager and the editors of *Prevention* magazine, *The Doctors Book of Food Remedies*, 31.

66. Arja T. Erkkilä, David M. Herrington, Dariush Mozaffarian, and Alice H. Lichtenstein, "Cereal Fiber and Whole-Grain Intake Are Associated With Reduced Progression of Coronary-Artery Atherosclerosis in Postmenopausal Women With Coronary Artery Disease," *American Heart Journal* 150, no. 1 (July 2005), 94–101, http://www.ahjonline.com/article/S0002 -8703(04)00507-1/abstract (accessed February 4, 2009).

67. Rafael de Cabo, PhD, Aging, Metabolism, and Nutrition Unit, Laboratory of Experimental Gerontology, http:// www.grc.nia.nih.gov/branches/leg/amnu.htm (accessed February 6, 2009).

68. Tyler Parr, "Insulin Exposure and Unifying Aging," *Gerontology* 45, no. 3 (May/June 1999): 121–135.

69. María I. Gil, Francisco A. Tomás-Barberán, Betty Hess-Pierce, et al., "Antioxidant Activity of Pomegranate Juice and Its Relationship With Phenolic Composition and Processing," *Journal of Agricultural and Food Chemistry* 48, no. 10 (2000): 4581–4589.

70. Salahuddin Ahmed, Naizhen Wang, Bilal Bin Hafeez, et al., "*Punica granatum L.* Extract Inhibits IL-1ß Induced Expression of Matrix Metalloproteinases by Inhibiting the Activation of MAP Kinases and NF- B in Human Chondrocytes In Vitro," *Journal of Nutrition* 135 (2005): 2096–2102, viewed at http://jn.nutrition.org/cgi/content/ full/135/9/2096 (accessed March 9, 2009).

71. H. M. Kwak, S. Y. Jeon, B. H. Sohng, et al., "Beta-Secretase (BACE1) Inhibitors From Pomegranate Husk," *Archives Pharmacal Research* 28 (2005): 1328–1332.

72. Phyllis A. Balch, *Prescription for Nutritional Healing*, third edition (New York: Avery, 2000), 74.

73. S. C. Larsson, E. Giovannucci, and A. Wolk, "A Prospective Study of Dietary Folate Intake and Risk of Colorectal Cancer: Modification by Caffeine Intake and Cigarette Smoking," *Cancer Epidemiology Biomarkers and Prevention* 14, no. 3 (March 2005): 740–743.

74. Inna I. Kruman, T. S. Kumaravel, Althaf Lohani, et al., "Folic Acid Deficiency and Homocysteine Impair DNA Repair in Hippocampal Neurons and Sensitize Them to Amyloid Toxicity in Experimental Models of Alzheimer's Disease," *Journal of Neuroscience* 22, no. 5 (March 1, 2002): 1752–1762, http://www.jneurosci.org/cgi/content/full/22/5/1752 (accessed April 13, 2009).

75. National Toxicology Program, "Draft NTP Brief on Bisphenol A," National Institute of Environmental Health Sciences National Institutes of Health, U.S. Department of Health and Human Services, April 14, 2008, http://cerhr.niehs.nih.gov/chemicals/bisphenol/BPADraftBriefVF_04_14_08.pdf (accessed February 9, 2009).

76. NBCWashington.com, "FDA Releases Report on Chemical Found in Plastics," September 3, 2008, Voxant Newsroom, http://www.thenewsroom.com/details/2993185/Health (accessed April 16, 2009).

77. Q. W. Shen, C. S. Jones, N. Kalchayanand, et al., "Effect of Dietary-lipoic Acid on Growth, Body Composition, Muscle Ph, and AMP-Activated Protein Kinase Phosphorylation in Mice," *Journal of Animal Science* 83, no. 11 (November 2005): 2611–2617.

78. Ana M. Andrade, Geoffrey W. Greene, and Kathleen J. Melanson, "Eating Slowly Led to Decreases in Energy Intake Within Meals in Healthy Women," *Journal of the American Dietetic Association* 108, no. 7 (July 2008): 1186–1191, http://www.adajournal.org/article/S0002-8223(08)00518-X/abstract (accessed April 13, 2009).

79. Maoshing Ni, "Top Seven Ways to Beat Holiday Bloat," Yahoo! Health, November 24, 2008, http://health.yahoo.com/experts/drmao/16795/top-7-ways-beat-holiday-bloat/ (accessed March 5, 2009).

80. National Cancer Institute, " Heterocyclic Amines in Cooked Meats," National Cancer Institute FactSheet, http://www.cancer.gov/cancertopics/factsheet/Risk/ heterocyclic-amines (accessed March 9, 2009).

81. John W. Anderson and Larry Trivieri, eds., *Alternative Medicine: The Definitive Guide* (n.p.: Ten Speed Press, 2002), 801.

82. "Forgive to Live," *Health* magazine, July/August 2000, 28.

83. Leah R. Garnett, "Taking Emotions to Heart—Emotions and Coronary Disease," *Harvard Health Letter*, October 1996.

84. Institute for Health Psychology, San Diego; Joe Spira, PhD, Director.

85. Pamela M. Peeke, MD, MPH, "Don't Postpone Joy," Prevention.com, http://www.prevention.com/cda/article/ don-t-postpone-joy/656a72e50d803110VgnVCM100000 13281eac____/health/emotional.health (accessed March 9, 2009).

86. Les Parrott and Leslie Parrott, *Relationships: How to Make Bad Relationships Good* (Grand Rapids, MI: Zondervan, 2002), 15.

87. James S. House, "Social Isolation Kills, but How and Why?" *Psychosomatic Medicine* 63 (2001): 273–274.

88. W. R. Stricklin, "Space as an Environmental Enrichment," *Laboratory Animals* 24, no. 4 (1995): 24–27.

89. WisdomQuotes.com, "Kenneth Patton Quotes," http:// www.wisdomquotes.com/000275.html (accessed February 17, 2009).

90. Maoshing Ni, *Secrets of Longevity: Hundreds of Ways to Live to Be 100* (San Francisco: Chronicle Books, 2006), 300.

91. Great-Quotes.com, "Eleanor Roosevelt Quotes," http://www.great-quotes.com/ cgi-bin/viewquotes.cgi?action=search&Author_First_ Name=Eleanor&Author_Last_Name=Roosevelt&Movie= (accessed March 25, 2009).

92. QuotationsPage.com, "Quotations by Author: William Penn," http://www.quotationspage.com/quotes/ William_Penn/ (accessed February 18, 2009).

93. Richard Foster, *Celebration of Discipline* (San Francisco: HarperCollins, 1998), 191.

94. These four steps were adapted from Rhonda Britton, "The Wheel of Freedom," in *Fearless Living* (n.p.: Perigee Trade, 2002).

95. ThinkExist.com, "Abraham Lincoln Quotes," http://thinkexist.com/quotation/the_better_part_of_one-s_life_consists_of_his/145509.html (accessed February 19, 2009).

96. Janet Maccaro, *Breaking the Grip of Dangerous Emotions* (Lake Mary, FL: Siloam, 2001, 2005), 143–144.

97. Des Cummings Jr. and Monica Reed, "Trust in Divine Power," in *Creation Health Discovery: God's Guide to Health and Healing* (n.p.: Florida Hospital Publishing, 2005), 65.

98. Ibid., 63.

99. Famous Quotes and Authors, "William Ralph Inge Quotes and Quotations," http://www.famousquotesandauthors.com/authors/william_ralph_inge_quotes.html (accessed March 6, 2009).

100. T. D. Jakes, *The Lady, Her Lover, and Her Lord* (New York: Putnam, 1998), 19.

101. S. Fulder, M. Kataria, and B. Gethyn-Smith, "A Double Blind Clinical Trial of Panax Ginseng in Aged Subjects," presented at the Fourth International Ginseng Symposium, Daejon, Korea, September 18–20, 1984.

Readers who enjoyed this book will also enjoy

100 Answers to 100 Questions about God

100 Answers to 100 Questions about God's Promises

100 Answers to 100 Questions about Loving Your Husband

100 Answers to 100 Questions about Loving Your Wife

100 Answers to 100 Questions about Prayer

100 Answers to 100 Questions to Ask Before You Say "I Do"

100 Answers to 100 Questions about Being a Great Mom

100 Answers to 100 Questions about Being a Great Dad

100 Answers to 100 Questions Every Graduate Should Know